The Successful Employee

Proven, Practical Methods to Advance Your Career

Victor Illian

No part of this book may be reproduced, transmitted, or sold in whole or in part in any form without prior explicit written permission from the author or Set Forward Publishing LLC. All trademarks and registered trademarks included in this book are the property of their respective owners.

Some information included in this book is from third party sources. Inclusion of third party materials is an expression of the author's own recommendation and opinion of said material. The author and Set Forward Publishing LLC provides no guarantee of success of any kind to the reader from application of any information, instruction, opinion, products, or services contained within this book. The methods and ideas discussed in this book do produce results but results will vary as they depend on many unique circumstances, work situations, and diligence of the reader. Some material in this book may be repurposed to appear in other publications including but not limited to blog posts, interviews, video, podcast, book excerpt, and other forms of digital or print media. Links included either within this book or from websites linked to may be or contain affiliate links. The author may receive compensation from an ultimate purchase resulting from use of such a link.

The author is not a financial, legal, or health professional and may at times provide opinions of financial, legal, health or other potential actions. Such advice are simply the recommendation and opinion of the author. The reader is strongly encouraged to seek out appropriate professional advice before attempting to apply any such advice. By reading this book you agree the author and Set Forward Publishing LLC are not responsible for the success or failure of your decisions relating to any information included in this book.

Copyright © 2017 by Set Forward Publishing LLC.
All rights reserved.

Learn more on the website: www.setforwardpublishing.com

ISBN: 1975749383
ISBN-13: 978-1975749385

DEDICATION

To my lovely wife, Becky, for always believing, always trusting, always encouraging. Thank you for providing the best, honest feedback.

And to my wonderful children for their inquisitive inspiration that presses me forward.

CONTENTS

	Acknowledgments	i
	Preface	3
1	What Does it Mean to Be a Successful Employee?	6
2	Risks of Not Trying to Be a Better Employee	12
3	Benefits of Being a Better Employee	18
4	Get the Basics Down	27
5	Build Up Your Character	31
6	Get and Stay Organized	48
7	Goals Management	75
8	Relate Well to Others	81
9	Expand Your Domain	105
10	Advance Your Work	123

ACKNOWLEDGMENTS

Thank you to everyone willing to be interviewed for this book for providing such amazing answers. This book would not be the same without the influential dynamic each of you has brought to the reader!

PREFACE

Who is This Book For?

Is this book right for you? Are you about to start on a new career in the workforce? Have you been in the workforce for a while but want to breathe new life into your career?

When we step out of high school or college into the working world, often our education has really only provided knowledge. While knowledge is crucial to any career, what about an actual roadmap to success? When you finished your last class, did you breathe a sigh of relief saying how glad you were that your school provided you actionable steps to navigate your way in the professional world? I did not. I received a good education, but nothing about how to effectively chart my course into my chosen field.

When handed that diploma or certificate of completion, you are off - off to face the challenges of crafting your course through work on your own. This can be a liberating and exciting feeling. But it can also leave one feeling a bit anxious.

What if you had more?

What if you had some words of wisdom from those that stepped through that door of opportunity in life before you? A roadmap. A guidebook. Something to hold in your hand as you step forward to chart the course you so eagerly wish to embark on.

What if you have been in the workforce for a while now but you long to step up your game? To stand out among others in your profession. Be noticed.

If any of this resonates, YOU are why this book was created!

Throughout this book you will see quotes from people that care about your success as an employee. People willing to take time from their own successful careers to provide real wisdom for your benefit. These employees have been carefully selected in recognition of their pursuit of being just what you are looking for. The successful employee.

Take this journey with us.

I'm excited for what I'm confident will grow in your career as a result of seeds planted by this book! This isn't so much a book as it is a connection, an introduction to a dialogue. A dialogue between you, me, and others reading this book. Why? Because any successful roadmap can only truly become successful once it is put into action. Action takes support. You aren't working at a career alone in a vacuum. You are at this alongside each of us. Shoulder to shoulder pushing forward. So why do it alone? Each one of us has unique insights and perspectives that can benefit the other in our common mission. So let's do just that!

To get the best possible outcomes from this book involve others in your journey! Join me and other readers of this book at www.successlifter.com/the-successful-employee. Let's help each other advance our career and become the successful employee we each seek to become.

Ready to start this journey with me?

You've got this! Let's go!

1. WHAT DOES IT MEAN TO BE A SUCCESSFUL EMPLOYEE?

When embarking on any life mission it is a good idea to solidify your understanding of what you are after and why. This may seem silly to you at first. I mean, you already know you want to be a more successful employee, right? So why do you need to define this for yourself?

It can be hard to keep the entire picture of what we want to achieve in the front of our minds all at once, all the time. Especially if we use a subjective label like "success." Ask any two people what success means to them in their lives and you will get different answers. Sure, there may be some similarities, but the success definition is unique to the individual.

If you are anything like me you may be feeling excited to get started on this new endeavor right now. To jump right in with both feet. Like jumping into the swimming pool without checking the water temperature or depth first. You want to experience. You want to advance. You want to realize your goals as fast as possible. I'm with you.

Maybe you aren't one to jump right into the water with both feet. Do you prefer to dip your toe in and think about if it is worth it or not, calculating the possible risks? Did you eat too recently? Maybe you will get a cramp if you swim right now. Questioning and evaluating before you get started is a great thing to do. I've found myself too far on this side at times though as well. Questioning things until I realize I have taken absolutely no action and maybe never will. Fear sets in and I retreat to my comfort zone, surrounding myself with a veil of rationalized arguments to justify why I can't move forward.

Before we dive into that inviting pool let's get crystal clear about what we are hoping to achieve here. Take a step back. Close your eyes. Take a deep calming breath. Now think. What does it means to be a successful employee? Not someone else's definition; your definition. Make this thought very real. See yourself walking into your place of employment. What are you wearing? How do you feel about your job? How do you feel about your boss? Do you like where the company is headed?

Now picture yourself taking your station or sitting at your desk; getting started with your day. What things happen during the day? How do you react to each one? If you picture yourself responding in a way you don't like, retrace that thought and make a new one. Think of what the rest of the day would look like with a success-oriented reaction.

Picture yourself talking to your boss; talking to the owner of the company. What are those conversations like?

Practice seeing yourself being the successful employee you want to be.

> **EXERCISE**
>
> Devote a fresh notebook to document this journey. Based on the exercise above, begin with a paragraph or so describing what it means to you to be a successful employee. Read over what you wrote. Add a bullet list, based on your paragraph, with each of the characteristics of a successful employee that you wish to gain. In bold letters above your bullet list write, "GOALS". This book was created to help you expand on these goals. To give you actionable tools to start achieving them.

If you find it hard to build out your list of goals, the following may also help. Several employees building great careers offered their definition of what it means to be a successful employee. I've included those below. Read through them and see what you resonate with. Take what fits your vision of success in your career and use it to build that goals list.

> *"Job security; Above-average interactions and relationships with co-workers; Being viewed and approached as a knowledgeable resource to others."*
> *- April Scrimger*

The Successful Employee

"Competence at the task, positive attitude, and a desire to continuously improve."

- Bradlee Clegg

"To me it means earning the respect of my superiors and making an impact on the business of my company. If I can communicate issues I see and reduce overhead in myself or my team's workflow that helps the company get more from us and reduces the cognitive load on us. I have seen a single developer become world renowned in the Android development space simply from making excellent tools that reduce the amount of work other developers need to do manually. If you can make a similar impact in your company that is huge. Ultimately though, I define success in my job as being able to accomplish the most in the time I'm at work and not letting it bleed over into my personal life."

- C.J. Gonzalez

"A successful employee is one who is trustworthy, reliable, and invested in making the company successful. They work at developing relationships at all levels and leverage those relationships for their personal development."

- Fran Mosher

"It means that you are contributing to your [company's] success, but at the same time remaining happy yourself."

- Garrick Woodberry

"One who exceeds the expectations of the given job description."
 - Ernest Randall Taylor

"Enjoying my work, taking pride in it and doing the best I can. Earning the respect of my coworkers and supervisors. Being able to take constructive criticism, knowing it will help better myself. Own up to your mistakes and learn from them."
 - Ellen Coppler

"I think a successful employee is someone who has a great attitude, stays on top of their work, treats others with respect."
 - Matthew Donaldson

"Being a successful employee is someone who brings a positive impact to themselves and the company/employer they work for."
 - Michael Grenzicki

"Being a successful employee means to me that all my hard work has meant something to someone. It's not just a paycheck. I also like being part of a winning team, in working together much can be achieved. And it also means that I have earned the trust of other people through developing and practicing my communication skills."
 - Rebecca Elliott

> *"Someone who goes above and beyond to deliver, no matter what it takes, long weekends, late nights.... Can do attitude."*
>
> *- Julie Bolinger*

You may not relate to some of these perspectives and that is okay. We are each individuals driven by individual objectives in life. Take time to think about what it is that drives you. What makes you want to get up in the morning? What makes you want to face the next day? Understanding what motivates you starts with understanding your specific personality. It can be hard to pinpoint your personality type and your key motivators so I've put together resources to help you in this quest. To check them out head over to www.successlifter.com/the-successful-employee.

2. RISKS OF NOT TRYING TO BE A BETTER EMPLOYEE

Why go through all this work? What are some risks of not putting this effort in?

If you aren't looking for a new job and you are content with your job just like it is why bother, right? But what if your job changes? Your boss alters your workload to include new tasks you need to accommodate because the company doesn't have enough resources yet to bring in more help. Even worse, your boss needs to cut a position. Some tough choices need to be made about productivity levels of existing employees. These aren't fun situations.

But they are very real. While it may sound cold and calculative these are real business decisions management needs to face. Productivity levels of employees. Employee engagement in their work. Commitment to the company. There are many hard choices a manager has to make. One of the hardest is which employee to let go because the company instructed a position be cut. While it is true you can't control that situation you have a great deal of control over how you present yourself to the company and your boss. Why not give yourself the best possible opportunity of showing yourself to be an essential employee to the company?

The biggest factor to keep in mind is control versus chance. How much control over your career do you want? How much of your career do you want to leave to chance?

So, what are some risks of not trying? Let's take a look at what others in the workforce said about this:

> *"The risk of being either overlooked, or targeted."*
> *- Ernest Randall Taylor*

> *"You may get overlooked for various promotions. It may follow you on when you decide to move on and your new companies are doing reference checks."*
> *- Garrick Woodberry*

> *"Little or no opportunity for career advancement; no merit raises based on work quality and/or attitude; being an outcast among your peers; not viewed as [a] go-to person or someone to whom new challenges/duties are given."*
> *- April Scrimger*

"Management tends to unconsciously and consciously categorize employees. Accordingly, prime work opportunities and higher pay achievement are affected by an employee's perceived engagement. Once an employee has gained a poor reputation or been pigeon-holed by their work engagement (behavior), it is difficult to change the perspective. The phrase "trying to be a better employee" calls to mind the word "lackluster". Lackluster doesn't get anyone far in the business world."

- Fran Mosher

"I think one of the main risks is you may get overlooked when applying for a promotion or new position at your place of employment."

- Matthew Donaldson

"Complacency - doing the same old thing, or just going through the motions - will eventually cause you to fall behind or make critical mistakes. It will eventually get noticed, and if you are making someone else work harder, they will look to fix the problem, either by working with you to fix it, or more likely, by removing you from the organization. Even if the lackluster performance goes unnoticed, it will likely make your job harder in the future."

- Bradlee Clegg

> *"I work in an industry that moves at a faster pace than most. In an environment like that the risk of stagnating is that your skills will become outdated and less relevant. Finding jobs would become much harder. You also run the risk of developing a reputation of being a complacent employee, many managers know each other between companies and a bridge burnt in one company may follow you further than you think."*
>
> *- C.J. Gonzalez*

> *"You risk flatlining and being stuck in a Groundhog Day state. Doing the same repetitive task everyday. Your fellow employees will realize that you don't want anything better for yourself which is just hurting the company and then they will lose interest in helping you or even working with you. You will in essence be an anchor on a ship. Which if the company feels you become too much of an anchor will let you go at which point you will be looking for a job for a person that was better when they hit the job market but now shows no enthusiasm."*
>
> *- Michael Grenzicki*

Those are good reasons to not leave your career to chance. Rather to take control. Control over your job, your career. Not leaving everything to chance. I'm sure at least one person reading this might be saying, what a minute, there is no way you can control everything in your career and certainly not the big things out of your hands. For instance, if you are pursuing a job with Google. You can't make them hire you.

That's fair. I agree you can't really control if someone else will do anything and by no means am I suggesting this book can guarantee you will land your dream job or that your boss will say yes to your requests. But I can say that the more of your career you take control of instead of leaving to chance the more likely things working out in your favor becomes. While you may not be able to guarantee Google will hire you, what you can do is make yourself as appealing a candidate as possible.

Want to get noticed by a company? Make them see you know what their goals are and what difficulties they face. How do you do that? Research the company. Before you even send your resume, learn all you can about the company from the internet. Specifically look for media announcements from the company alluding to current goals and possible challenges the company faces. Then, think about ways you can help them move forward in their plan.

Forbes posted results from a National Association of Colleges and Employers (NACE) survey which listed the *"ability to make decisions and solve problems"* as the number two skill employers seek. The number one was the *"ability to work in a team."* (Adams)

Show them you know where they are headed as a company and how you can help them in that direction. Include this on your cover letter to your resume. This is your first opportunity to sell yourself to your prospective employer.

Does all this sounds like it could be a lot of work? A lot of work that you don't know will result in the win you want? Influencing the people around you toward favorable decisions is never a guarantee but it is worth the effort. I hope this quote from a great work colleague of mine will bring you more hope in this endeavor.

The Successful Employee

"To choose a path of 'just good enough,' taking satisfaction in avoiding opportunities to stretch ourselves, or allowing a fear of failure to prevent our professional development leaves us in a grey twilight of mediocrity. To quote former President of the United States Theodore Roosevelt, 'Far better is it to dare mighty things, to win glorious triumphs, even though checkered by failure... than to rank with those poor spirits who neither enjoy nor suffer much, because they live in a gray twilight that knows not victory nor defeat.'"

- Torin Lucas

3. BENEFITS OF BEING A BETTER EMPLOYEE

One question you may have been asking yourself is, "Why?" Why bother going through the work of being a better employee? In the last section we talked about some possible risks of not trying. Now let's look at some potential benefits to working toward becoming a better employee.

> *"To me, being a better employee equals being a better person."*
>
> *- Ernest Randall Taylor*

It is in the doing of our lives that we will find professional fulfillment. A sense of success, self-worth and community may all stem from striving toward our employment excellence. While the work we do should not be the only source of fulfillment, it is an important area from which we derive meaning and direction in our lives. You will find that as you strive and grow as an employee you will find rewards richer than those of simple monetary value, though financial rewards are important too.

The Successful Employee

"Many of us find ourselves in work which challenges our sense of worth, we question whether we add value to our team, invariably we have setbacks, failures and occasions to lose heart. But an undaunted spirit of professional improvement both in and outside our workplace will pave the path forward. The prize fighter gets another chance and as we seek to ready ourselves for the next fight we strengthen our professional muscle and sense of self purpose."

— *Torin Lucas*

Well, first I would like to eventually advance whether within the company I'm with or be able to move onto another firm. Being a better employee, helps the employer trust the employee with more important tasks, giving the employee experience and skill development.

"Let me state the obvious benefit first, hopefully being a better employee would earn one either some sort of bonus or pay increase. Other benefits would be to gain experience, to learn how to interact with others and then the feeling of accomplishment."

— *Rebecca Elliott*

> *"I try to be a better employee to first and foremost benefit myself and my life and second to benefit my employer. The benefit for myself is to get better at what I do, which may lead to job security, better pay, better benefits, an overall happier lifestyle, and if the need arises a better resume. If I am better it gives me a chance to be the frontrunner on new tasks with my employer instead of doing the same thing day in and day out. I try to be a better employee for my employer so the company I work for grows and thrives. If the employees for a company don't want to be better how can the company ever become better? Making myself better makes the company better which leads to new exciting opportunities which changes the everyday. You have tasks to look forward to and new challenges to try and overcome, which in the end if the company thrives I thrive too."*
> *- Michael Grenzicki*

> *"There are various benefits to being a better employee depending on what company you are employed by. If you are employed by a decent company who acknowledges work, one may be to receive recognition."*
> *- Garrick Woodberry*

Better Pay

If you want to increase the amount you are paid, demonstrate to your boss and the company that your work is worth the extra money. Think in terms of your employer. You are an investment. All investments need to show some type of return. Your employer has invested time, money, and other resources into you as an employee. They want a favorable return on that investment. And rightly so.

> *"There is a sense of pride you can take in your work. For me there is a satisfaction knowing that that there is a field [in which] I can use personal skills to contribute to a cause greater than myself. A major motivating factor for improving your skills to stay relevant is the financial compensation provided by your employer. The more relevant your skills, the higher you're compensated and the better or more interesting the projects you get to work on."*
>
> *- C.J. Gonzalez*

Using this book, you can strategically plan ways to improve your value to the company, making you a greater asset. Document your progress in these areas to use as backing when you go to speak to your boss about a raise.

EXERCISE

Open your notebook and start two lists.

For the first list, write out each notable accomplishment you have within the past six months.

Then for the second list, write out each accomplishment you plan to achieve within the next six months.

> *"You'll want to be able to demonstrate that your presence adds value or makes the company more profitable. Make a strong case on paper for why you deserve a raise. Show tangible accomplishments."*
> — *How to Get a Raise, Wall Street Journal*

Better Position

> *"To be a valued and trusted member of your own departmental team; viewed as dependable and capable; serve as a go-to resource for others; as a means to be promoted to better career opportunities."*
> — *April Scrimger*

> *"When you try to be a better employee you get more self-fulfillment out of your job. It also helps you maintain a more positive attitude throughout the day, which improves relationships. There are also more advancement opportunities since employers promote the better employees."*
> — *Ellen Coppler*

Pay may not be your motivator or not your only motivator. Being given more favorable work is another great reason for seeking to better yourself as an employee.

> *"While 'better' is a subjective term, it implies working to better the company, i.e., being engaged in the business. Better employees typically are more productive and thereby gain the attention (and hopefully the compensation) of management. Promotability is closely linked to having the attention of management, often eliciting a 'career champion.' Some of the benefits derived are higher compensation, meaningful work assignments, and individual attention."*
>
> *- Fran Mosher*

Similar to the objective of better pay, you will do well to keep track of areas you bring value to the company you work for. Not just in line with your own objectives but especially the objectives of the company. Don't be afraid to document these accomplishments and present this during your meeting with management. Focus on presenting this information not as bragging rights but honest, objective, and measured data on what you have already and are currently bringing to the company.

Go into this meeting prepared. Not just your documentation but also you. Rehearse what you plan to say. What will management likely say in return and how will you react? Done right, this meeting can position you well to ask for specific changes to the work you do for the company. Demonstrate the value you bring to the company already. Make sure they recognize your current value, then demonstrate the increased value you could be providing should these changes go into effect. It will then be far easier for management to see how much value you could bring in a position where your talents are better utilized.

Perks

Company car. More autonomy in setting a work schedule that better fits your life. I'm sure you can think of many more perks than these. Perks specific to your company and your own situation. Don't be afraid to ask and maybe even negotiate some so this benefits both you and the company.

EXERCISE

In your notebook, start a list of perks that you would like from your career or from your current job.

Write out everything that comes to your mind.

Don't hold any back. Get them all on paper.

Go back over your list and circle the top few you want to attain first.

"I think some people just have the desire to be the best employee that they can be. I think the benefits to being a better employee are the possibility of promotion, and sometimes a little more slack with your boss."
- Matthew Donaldson

"Internally as a person you feel a sense of self gratification. A good example to me is when you have worked hard in your yard all day planting and arranging your garden then the rewards of how your hard effort pay off. Yes you are tired but the output is so gratifying and inside you are restful knowing that you did a good job. I feel this is the same in the workplace, the more you put in as an employee the more gratification you will receive from your efforts invested."
- Julie Bolinnger

Career Path

Certainly a key reason to better oneself as an employee is if you have a specific career path in mind. Depending on the company you work at, advancement within the company may need to be initiated by you. While some companies may actively encourage employees to step forward, show initiative, and take on new roles to expand their duties, not all companies function this way. Some organizations will wait to see if you demonstrate a desire for advancement before even considering if you have a potential for advancement. In either case, taking the first step to actively pursue advancement may put a bit more control in your favor.

Not all career paths involve advancements within the same company. Many companies you work for along your career path may actually be strategic moves to acquire the experience or contacts needed to advance into the company you are after.

An example may be attaining a senior developer position at Microsoft or Google. Getting an entry-level programming job at Google may be feasible right out of college, but they may not be willing to hire entry-level skills at the time you apply. Rather than giving up on your career path, working a couple years at a smaller development firm may be the step needed to advance into a higher-level role at Google.

> *"I believe in trying to be a better employee for several reasons. There is a sense of pride in doing a good job that is its own reward, that leads to a [sense] of self-respect and self-worth, no matter what the task is. I also am a person of faith. I believe that in all you do, do it for the Lord, and if you are faithful in the little things, he is faithful in the big things. However, the most practical reason is that supervisors really do notice. Excellence (or even competence, sometimes) leads to opportunities to advance."*
>
> *- Bradlee Clegg*

> *"I've received numerous. . .awards, raises and better employment. Your track record follows you. So if you [are] a solid employee at a lower tier company hopefully it will translate to your real career in the future."*
>
> *- Garrick Woodberry*

4. GET THE BASICS DOWN

We talked about reasons why you would want to put the effort in. The effort to becoming a better employee. You may even be ready to dig right in and work on some core areas. But first we need to set a baseline. We need to build a foundation to work with.

Any of the core areas we try to lay onto a weak foundation will likely not be nearly as effective. What do I mean by this foundation and these core areas? This chapter is intended to build a good foundation. A good starting point that we will put more methods on top of. The core areas are those methods we are going to be building on top of the concepts in this chapter.

With that, let's get going on our foundation.

Dress Appropriately

How we dress communicates much about our readiness to work, our consideration of others, and our willingness to abide by policies set out by the company. While not all jobs require specific, uniformed attire, many have clearly documented directives on what is and is not appropriate for apparel in the workplace. Our willingness to observe these policies is one of the first ways others will evaluate our desire to help the company advance.

Be sure to find out what the dress code policy is at your workplace. If you aren't sure where to find this, ask your manager or the Human Resources department for more information on the company's dress code.

Some organizations offer days where the standard dress code is relaxed. When participating in such days consider what you choose so as to not push the limits further than seems appropriate.

Certainly it may be easy within your organization to find loopholes or ways you can manage to wear what you want and still be within the letter of the company policy so to speak. The policy says nothing about ironing your clothes so that shirt you pulled out of the closet this morning covered in wrinkles is perfectly fine, right? The concert t-shirt with printed words your mom would have stopped you right in your tracks if you tried to wear to school when you were a kid. There is nothing in the policy specifically about those.

Before you pull either of those shirts over your head ask yourself what message you are sending to your employer, to your boss, to your coworkers. Is it a message that supports the employee you want them to see you as?

No Inappropriate Language

"While coarse language may be acceptable in some settings, it never serves the successful employee well."
- Fran Mosher

This may seem like common sense, but my experience with various employees across many companies has proven otherwise. Have you ever worked at a company where vulgar, obscene, and inappropriate conversations were considered commonplace and acceptable? Maybe this isn't a big deal for some if you are not actively participating in the conversation, but what happens when customers begin to overhear?

One such company I worked for expressed no concern regarding how appropriate employee conversations were. Since employees were allowed to talk however they wanted to each other, the impact it had on customers went unnoticed by the management. Drop-in visit customers or customers calling over the phone could hear these background conversations in detail. What impression of this company do you think those overheard conversations left for the customers?

Opposition to this viewpoint is to be expected. Having to watch what we say is not favorable to all. And some merit can be found in this freedom to speak to team members in ways that create a cohesive team bond.

A Forbes article brings to light something of both sides to this argument. The article quotes a CareerBuilder.com study reporting 81% of employers surveyed believe swearing at work brings into question an employee's professionalism. The article goes on to provide an insightful explanation of the power of words - a power to build others up or to tear them down. (Nordstrom)

Another such work environment I experienced demonstrated the negative power of words, not only on me, but peers at the company as well. When the outcome from a task was unfavorable, management would react by verbally belittling the employee with sharply coarse and profane language. This had a great deal of negative impact on morale within the company. A negative impact that eventually led, at least in part, to me and several others at that organization seeking employment elsewhere.

Ultimately the choice belongs to each of us on what words we choose to use and what outcome we seek from our speech. Knowing the effect our words can have provides us insight to steer conversations in desirable ways.

Treat Others With Respect

As with any interactions with others we have in life, our daily communications with our coworkers and managers should always maintain respect for the other person. Breaking this cardinal rule can be of great detriment to one's career. While these ramifications may not be realized in the short term, the impact could deliver a critical blow over time.

A simple and effective solution to this is to treat others around you with the respect you hope they would offer you. Consistently applying this mantra will reap benefits to you even if only in the respect you see returned upon you.

5. BUILD UP YOUR CHARACTER

"Read books, listen to podcasts, or watch videos related to management and workplace culture. Establish a LinkedIn profile and try to read at least one article a week to keep current on business items of discussion. Seek out a mentor who can encourage and provide guidance in being successful. There also may be some classes at a Community College that would be helpful. A number of years ago I taught a class at the New Mexico Junior College entitled 'Professional Development'. It was a mandatory class for receiving an Associate's Degree. My approach was to provide my students with as much exposure to the business world as possible. One of the primary assignments given these students was to conduct an interview with a business owner or someone they considered a success and write a one page summary about what they learned. The goal was to demonstrate that the path to success is varied. Individuals can do this for themselves. The targeted Interviewee is always flattered to be asked about their successes."

- Fran Mosher

"Mentorship. Seek someone to emulate."
- Ernest Randall Taylor

Did you know your character is really something you define? That may seem like a simple and obvious statement, but I think it can be overlooked. Do we always consider the impact an action we take will have on our character before we take action? How would your character look different if you considered the results each time you were about to act? This isn't about pleasing others and looking good to them. This is about establishing the core character you want others to see you possess, the core character you want to possess.

That can be a tough question. I have not always made the choice I wished I had looking back. Had I taken time to consider the outcomes of some of those choices, I would have made a different choice.

> *"Make success a part of your character - always behave in ways that show you are working towards excellence. Not for the sake of being noticed by a superior, but so that you know that you are a success."*
>
> *- Bradlee Clegg*

> *"Ask questions and seek to fully understand what is assigned to ensure the final product is as intended. Don't pretend to know an answer that you don't know but be willing to seek out the answer. Ask for other stakeholders' input to develop a clear understanding of variables for a given project/topic. Follow through on your duties, commitments and deadlines. Be approachable - by all 'levels' of staff within an organization. Be friendly and have a sense of humor. Have good attendance."*
>
> *- April Scrimger*

Before we go any further, let's take just a moment to establish a good working definition of what character really is.

The Merriam-Webster dictionary defines character as *"One of the attributes or features that make up and distinguish an individual."* (Merriam-Webster)

The two factors that jumped out at me with this definition are "attributes/features" and "make up/distinguish an individual".

How do we establish or acquire these "attributes" and "features"? We build them! They become a reflection to others of what they can expect from us in various situations. They build a trust level based on past actions. We build this trust factor by being consistent with the positive ways we treat those around us. This is true for the big, hard decisions just as much as it is with the little everyday ones. They all serve to build up or tear down our character.

Put together these positive and negative interactions we have with others and they become the aspects that "make up" or "distinguish us as an individual" to others. Another way we could say that is, our actions train others what kind of character they should expect from us. Don't you want that expectation to be a good one?

You may be saying right now, this is all about perception. Why should I care about how others see me? Shouldn't I be concerned with how I live my life more than how others view me?

I do believe we should not get caught up in the perception of others to the point we become driven by pleasing them. That is not the goal of the above language. We won't please everyone all the time. Being kind and considerate to those around us is something we should certainly do, but living our lives with the purpose of pleasing others around us as our main focus can lead to disappointment.

Decide on the character you want to have. Internalize the vision of that character. Then allow it to influence your choices and interactions with others. Others will start seeing you the way you want them to see you.

Honest and Full of Integrity

> *"When you slack off or continuously don't try, you damage your reputation, not only with your superiors but with your peers as well. You risk the chance of being passed up for projects or advancement. You also miss out on networking opportunities."*
> *- Ellen Coppler*

> *"Don't sacrifice your sanity or happiness for a check. But if you decide to work with a company and you know their policy, do your best. Your work is a reflection of you and employers will judge you off your work ethic."*
> *- Garrick Woodberry*

Honesty and integrity are crucial elements to a good character. Your manager needs to know you are worthy of trust. Your co-workers need to know you are not going to turn your back on them when you agree to help them with a problem they face at work.

As with building up any character trait, consistency is key. Demonstrating your honesty in one or two situations followed by dishonesty will not foster trust. Your honesty and integrity must be consistent over time.

While these traits may seem simple to master, they could prove challenging given certain circumstances. Not directly lying about something to your boss may be pretty easy. What if the email server is brought down and it is reportedly due to a virus that infected the company network? It may not be as easy for an employee to admit it was due to opening a non-work related website from their desk computer which in turn infected the computer with the virus.

Honesty must be within each action we take as the slightest overtly dishonest act can undermine much work.

Self-Starter

> *"I think trying to go above and beyond when working on tasks has helped me to become a better employee. At least in the eyes of some of my past employers."*
>
> *- Matthew Donaldson*

> *"Reading articles online on what technologies and strategies other companies are using has been very useful in keeping abreast of the latest trends. Also my current company has provided access to Pluralsight (online video) tutorials covering a wide variety of topics that I can use to better my knowledge and skills. My manager has routine feedback in our 1-on-1s and pushes me to improve and tackle problems I have not faced before. Other employees I know participate in professional clubs like Toastmasters to work on public speaking."*
>
> *- C.J. Gonzalez*

Showing yourself willing to jump into something new at work, even without being asked or prompted first, can show your manager you want to contribute to the greater good of the company.

The Successful Employee

"I think the criteria to classify an employee as better than average would be if the employee goes above and beyond of what is expected to be done. I'm not saying to be taken advantage of, but to show interest and improve the overall experience of work. For example, take a process and improve on it."

- Garrick Woodberry

"Their drive and not only their ability to get things done but to get things done better than it was done yesterday. They may automate a repetitive task, they may ask if a task is needed anymore, they might research and learn a new skill to speed up a process. They are putting an extra effort in to make the company better. That extra effort might be time but it doesn't have to be. Willingness to learn, passion, enthusiasm, and different are some of the words I would use to describe the better than average employee."

- Michael Grenzicki

Is there a project you know no one on the team has the needed training for? You could research training options and present the cost breakdown to your manager for sending you to obtain this training so the team can move forward with the project.

Show yourself to be proactive to your boss when appropriate.

Modest

Does a guy running the machine press at work insist on making everyone know he is the most efficient worker at the company? Do you find it hard to compete with his speed and accuracy?

It can be hard to work with someone who thinks they know everything there is to possibly know about their job and likes to express that at any given moment. Just remember that no one else probably likes hearing about his stellar abilities being self-promoted every day either.

Announcing your own accomplishments to anyone willing to listen may not be the best way to get noticed. Yet, a degree of self-promotion to your boss can prove helpful to advance. Just be sure you are not coming across boastful so much as frank.

Keep track of your accomplishments at work to draw reference to them during key discussions with your manager. However, a good measure of modesty is advised for our day-to-day conversations with others. Modesty will ultimately serve you far better than daily advertising your skills and abilities.

Confident

While we don't want to come across arrogant, we also don't want to hide our capabilities. Demonstrate your confidence in your abilities when appropriate. When a need arises, be quick to offer your unique skills and talents to solve the problem.

Resist adding your own self-promoting words after providing needed support. Allow your actions to speak on their own behalf.

> *"I look for those employees who appear to be truly passionate about their work. People who get excited to do their work and get it done efficiently are usually those employees I try to emulate the most."*
>
> *- C.J. Gonzalez*

Reliable

> *"Keeping a great attitude. Meeting with Leadership and asking for help in areas where you struggle. Building positive working relationships with peers and customers. Being dependable, trustworthy and loyal."*
>
> *- Julie Bolinger*

A consistent chain of events where you have been willing to help outside of your duties or even just do what was expected of you improves others' view of your reliability. To say you will do something but then go back on your word as if it meant very little will leave others with the impression they may not be able to count on you next time.

Always give careful consideration to a commitment before you agree to it. What is the likelihood you will be able to deliver on your commitment?

There are times it is not possible to live up to the commitment you made to someone else. Situations beyond your control could have affected your means to meet the commitment. If this happens, go to the person as soon as possible and explain why you will not be able to fill your commitment. Leaving them wondering why you never did what you said could lead them to unfavorable conclusions about you.

> *"A better than average employee asks questions, volunteers or asks to be part of work projects, goes out of their way to help others, accepts responsibility for mistakes, and gives credit to others when warranted. They earn the title of being reliable and creative by their work ethic and productivity."*
> *- Fran Mosher*

> *"I look at work ethic and quality, then productivity. Someone who takes pride and ownership in their work. If [they are] eager to learn and better themselves and asks questions. Someone others turn to for help and advice."*
>
> *- Ellen Coppler*

Adaptive and Flexible

> *"Find what drives you and do it. Don't settle for a set schedule, change your day to day, ask questions, be passionate. Look for ways to improve your life, look at what you're doing and ask yourself how is this helping me? How is what I am doing going to make things better today, tomorrow and the next day? Is there another way to do it that would be better at a broader scale? Hold yourself accountable as well as others."*
> *- Michael Grenzicki*

There are very important things in our lives that we should not compromise on. There are also times we can overlook a minor inconvenience or shift in our schedule to help someone when needed. Being adaptive and flexible when possible and maintaining a good attitude will speak much to others about your good character.

Measure the importance of each request made of you against what it would affect in your schedule. If your schedule never has room for a request could you be overscheduled, leaving you inflexible?

If situations change within a project and the work you were doing needs some changes how adaptive are you to those changes? While projects do need tight, defined parameters around expected outcomes there is typically some variance within the project that could not have been seen at the onset.

> *"In the words of Winston Churchill, 'Never give in, never give in, never, never, never, never - in nothing, great or small, large or petty - never give in except to convictions of honor and good sense.'"*
> — *Torin Lucas*

Open to Positive and Negative Feedback

> *"No matter what you try and do, always give your best. In most cases it will be noticed. It's good to be a leader, but sometimes you need to follow. And remember, we're all on the same team, the team to keep and make this establishment a success."*
> — *Rebecca Elliott*

No one likes to be criticized. Or at least not at the moment. But it doesn't have to be a negative experience. As with many things you encounter in your daily work, view criticism as an opportunity.

> *"Be open minded. Seek to help implement change, even when difficult. Give and seek constructive feedback in [a] non-threatening manner. Look at how you can impact shared/company goals."*
> — *April Scrimger*

When someone is providing you feedback on your performance, give objective and honest thought to why they feel it important to bring it to your attention. Do you agree with the reasoning behind their argument? Do you understand their motivation in discussing this with you?

If you don't understand, ask. If someone is criticizing you with the efforts of improving an outcome you have control of, give their viewpoint serious consideration. Work to understand what they are trying to communicate to you.

Perhaps their motivation is non-constructive. You can determine this by remaining calm and listening to their arguments. Follow this up with some probing questions, being careful to not elicit an even stronger reaction. Your goal here is to dig a little deeper into their motivation for speaking out against you. Either you will start to see there is a positive intention backing their statements or they will (hopefully) start to see their objections are grounded in emotion more than fact. This may offer them an opportunity to reframe their statements.

Constructive criticism should be openly welcomed! Probe their intentions to find what you can learn from their statements and apply to improving your actions next time if needed. This doesn't have to be a hit on your character if you don't let it. We all make bad choices from time to time but our character is built up or brought low more in the decisions we make once we recognize and realize the consequences of our bad choices.

Avoids Gossip

Gossip is something like a weed; it can grow quickly. Give it opportunity and it will spread to every crevice it can reach, almost as though it has a life of its own. Once gossip is spread it can catch on and be hard to break.

> *"Find a career or job you enjoy and are passionate about. If you enjoy your work you are going to want to always give your best. Don't get sucked into office gossip and try to avoid the individuals with a negative attitude. Be organized, plan your tasks and day, that way you get more accomplished."*
> — *Ellen Coppler*

I was once associated with an organization challenged by gossip. Rumors were easily distributed and believed by some to be fact. This had a crippling effect on the organization and was cause for many hurt emotions among its membership.

I would venture a guess that many organizations have at one time or another been negatively affected by gossip. We can't control the actions of everyone within the company we work for. What can we ourselves do about gossip?

First it is important to be able to recognize gossip when you hear it. If you suspect what you are being told is gossip, try asking some questions to substantiate the claims. Do this with tact. But if what you hear is gossip, asking clarifying questions may be enough to stop it.

Once you are fairly sure what you are hearing is gossip, gracefully exit or change the conversation to something more appropriate. Make a conscious effort not to internalize or act on the gossip. Without making a conscious decision to set aside the disinformation, you risk it filtering into your thoughts about people or situations.

Takes Ownership of Mistakes

Mistakes are to be expected. In fact, to think someone should never make a mistake is unrealistic. This thinking should be avoided about others as well as about yourself. We all make mistakes. What is important is what we do about those mistakes.

Once a mistake is made, there are numerous ways it can be dealt with. One may think not dealing with the mistake is an option, but taking no action is still a choice. Your lack of acknowledgement creates an impression on others. Will that impression be consistent with the employee you want others to see you as?

As Matthew Torin says in his post for Entrepreneur.com:

> *"Reasonable people realize when a mistake has been made and more often than not, owning up to it solves the problem. Not owning up to it adds fuel to a spark and ignites a problem you may not be able to contain later. When a delivery is late, when your inventory system screws up, when you drop the ball and completely forget an important deadline or phone call, don't try to deny it. As soon as you realize it's you (or your staff) that's dropped the ball, don't make excuses."*
>
> *- Matthew Torin*

Outright denial is one approach. Perhaps a manager confronts a worker regarding the poor condition in which a machine press was left at the end of a shift. The worker could flatly lie and claim no responsibility. It should be obvious this is not the preferred method to improving yourself as an employee.

Admitting to a mistake is far more beneficial to building one's value as an employee. What is far greater still is how one learns from a mistake.

Perhaps instead of an outright denial the employee admits to the mistake but does nothing to correct the action from occurring again. Next week the issue is brought to the employee by the boss a second time. And the week following as well.

Continuing to make that same mistake and taking no actions to prevent it in the future is far worse than having made the mistake in the first place.

How could the worker have properly handled this situation? Rather than seeing this mistake as a setback, the employee could have seen a learning experience and even more an opportunity. An opportunity to create a good impression moving forward by taking the negative outcome of the mistake and building something positive out of it.

When confronted about the mistake, the employee could have promptly taken ownership, admitted to the mistake, and followed up with an explanation of his plans to ensure that same mistake will not occur again. This re-centers the manager's focus, seeing the employee as working to fix problems rather than causing new ones. No longer is the primary focus the mistake or the risk of being thought of as a neglectful employee. The focus has been rerouted to a positive and desirable outcome. The manager's attention now is on an improvement to performance initiated by the employee. When a problem arises, anticipate your manager's reaction. Be ready with a suitable course of action to recommend that will meet your manager's expectations before he or she directs you on how to fix the problem.

Taken further, perhaps over the following week, the employee develops a very specific plan for how the machine can be more efficiently prepared for the next shift. Having documented the procedure, he presents it to his manager. Over the following weeks the employee is training other workers on how to properly implement the procedure on other machinery. This provides the employee an excellent event to document and bring back to his manager's attention in the future once the employee wants to request a more desirable position.

Now not all mistakes lend themselves to this level of outcome, but if you are watchful, looking for opportunities where most would see failure only or challenge, it is likely these opportunities will present themselves.

Is this manipulation? Are we trying to control the actions of our managers or the company we work for? Not at all. Manipulation implies we are bending someone's will to meet our own, most likely against their own desires. This is creating a situation where both parties, the employee and the employer, benefit and get something more than they had. We should never feel manipulative when our actions are creating value for those around us through honest and reputable methods.

6. GET AND STAY ORGANIZED

> *"Create a task list either on paper or electronic. Plan out your day, if possible, set aside time to work on certain projects/tasks. Don't let your workspace get cluttered. Look ahead on your calendar so you can be prepared for meetings. Communicate on deadlines and know what the expectations are."*
>
> *- Ellen Coppler*

Getting organized. If not the number one method to becoming a better employee, it is certainly a top contender. Does this chapter and the thought of organizing your work intimidate you a bit? If so, I hope to ease you into becoming more organized. It doesn't have to be an arduous ritual that becomes mundane and lifeless. Think of being organized as a tool you wield just like any of the other skills and talents you have cultivated and nurtured in your career thus far.

Are you just starting out in your career, feeling fairly new and not yet equipped with a tool chest full of resources? That is actually a great place to be. Right from the beginning, you can implement steps that will assure you are working in an organized environment that promotes enhanced productivity.

Whether you are just starting out in your field of work or have been at some type of work, or even various types of work, for many years, the benefits of strategically applying steps to become more organized can produce noticeable and lasting results.

Now that I've hopefully set the stage well enough to whet your appetite for the benefits of organization, let's get right into it!

Organize Your Digital Workspace

Even if you don't consider yourself tech-savvy, you may find yourself working with computers in your current job or in a future job. At the very least you may have a smartphone in your pocket or purse right now. Smartphones are computers in and of themselves.

Being a technology guru is far from necessary to operate and benefit from computers and other devices. However, some degree of familiarity is needed to be successful with the devices in the digital age in which we live. I feel it is important to provide guidance for any uncomfortable with computers and other digital devices. Rather than doing the topic an injustice by attempting to address it here in this chapter, I've built a list of resources to guide you in building your digital comfort level. These resources can be found at www.successlifter.com/the-successful-employee.

> *"I am using OneNote to track meeting/project notes. In the past I used scanned documents, ledger pads and handling file folders."*
>
> *- Matthew Donaldson*

Files

Have you ever received a file from someone but couldn't find it when you really need it? Where should you look for the file? Was it emailed to you? Was it a printout that you left on your desk someplace? Did you save it to a folder on your computer, but you just can't recall where that folder could be now?

What if you find the file, but just aren't sure if it is the most recent version? Did you get an updated copy at some point?

Or maybe you know exactly where you saved the file, but when your computer crashed two months ago the file was lost.

Have you experienced any of these issues before? If not, you are either very fortunate or have already implemented some key steps to keep your files safe and accessible.

For those who have fallen victim to something listed above or want to ensure you won't be the next victim, let's look at what proactive steps we can take to stop this!

> *"Our team's tracking system for work items (Microsoft's Team Foundation Server) helps greatly by defining what I'm expected to accomplish and showing me what everyone else is working on in case I need to assist. I also organize thoughts and notes either in a physical notepad or in OneNote on my computer."*
>
> *- C.J. Gonzalez*

> *"I rely heavily on digital tools - online calendars synced with email, taking the time on the front end to organize digital documents so that they can be easily found and used in the future. For important documents that I must not lose - I tack them up next to my desk."*
>
> *- Bradlee Clegg*

Touch Once Then File. Anytime you receive a file or information you know needs to be referenced at a future date, save it someplace for easy access. Plan ahead on where that location will be. Try to have just one location for that type of information. You will want to organize files and information in a manner that makes sense to you so when it comes time you can retrieve them more easily. This could be by project or topic of information. Give this filing structure some thought to determine what will work best for you. Ask yourself how you would most naturally think to find this information three months from now and that should help you determine your filing system.

Version Awareness. Now that you have an understanding of what filing structure would suit you let's look at version controlling. Consider a situation where you received an email with a file attached. The file is an updated version to a document you received last year. You know you won't need to act on this document for the next few months, but you will need to know you have the most recent version when you do. You may also need to reference prior versions at some point in the future. Plus, you fully expect to get new versions of this file going forward.

Fortunately, you had implemented the touch once then file concept and know exactly where to find the first version of the document. Pulling up that folder, you then save the new version to it as well. But, since the file name may be the same you alter the file name of both copies by adding some type of label to indicate what version the document is. This label could be as simple as a version number like "_v1.0" and "_v2.0" or the actual date of the document. (Hint: If you aren't sure the date of the first version, you can use the file modified date which should be viewable in the folder details for that file.) This date could look something like this "2017.02.21". (Hint: When I add a date to a file, I typically add it in year.month.day format so if I sort by file name I get them in version order right away.)

Loss Prevention. Where you save all these files is very important, not just the filing structure you use to more easily locate a document, but also the volatility of the folder you are saving to. What do I mean by volatility? Ask yourself before you start using a specific location for your electronic filing system, will you be able to get these files back if the drive they are saved on malfunctions or crashes? Once a drive crashes it is hard or sometimes even impossible to recover the files that were saved to it. Find out if your company does regular backups of any computer drives within the company. Is your desktop or laptop computer regularly backed up? Could you start backing up your computer to another location regularly? Your company's technical team or network support team should be able to help you in answering these questions and even with setting up your computer to perform regular backups.

Another consideration is being able to use a network drive. Network drives are similar to storing a file on your computer, but network drives are located on larger servers that many in the company can access. Some companies offer network drives which you can access while in the office. Find out what backup routine your company offers for any network drive location you are considering and be sure to ask how you go about requesting files be retrieved from the most recent backup if this becomes necessary in the future.

Emails

Finding an email you received months ago can be equally as difficult without some type of filing system. Most email programs offer the ability to create folders for storing emails in the same way computers offer this for files. This means you don't have to live out of your inbox sifting through all the emails you thought may be important one day.

You can use the same touch once then file method described above for filing your emails as well. Since emails are dated, the version control concept is taken care of for you as you save all those emails for a similar conversation, work project, or person to the same folder. When you open the folder later you can sort them by date received and easily see just the emails you are after and in the order they were received.

Determining the best folder structure for your email system is the same process you used for files. Think about how you would most naturally look for an email in the future. Would it be by related project, person who sent the email, etc.?

As for loss prevention, many office-based email systems are regularly backed up. If emails are downloaded to your computer then you will need to ensure regular backups are completed. This is another instance of when checking with your network support or technical team is needed. They will be able to advise you if your emails are currently being backed up regularly and at what frequency. If they are not already being backed up, they should be able to offer advice and assistance to start doing so.

Another extension to the touch once idea is to try to deal with an email when you first look at it. We can all fall into the trap of going through emails for hours and realize we didn't get all the work done we intended to for the day. Perhaps a lot of work was accomplished through those emails, but the scheduled work you had on your list may fall behind from an unrestricted amount of email time. One way to manage this is to schedule when you will look at email. Decide how often you feel you need to check your email. Usually it shouldn't need to be every minute and probably not even every hour. If you get important emails needing immediate attention, you could decide ahead of time you will first look at an email to see if it needs to be addressed right now or if it can wait until your scheduled email time. If it doesn't need your attention right now, wait until your scheduled time. Train yourself to follow this model should you choose to implement it. It will get you in the habit of better structuring your email time so as to not eat into your other work.

An approach I have found helpful is to clear my email inbox during the time I schedule to work through emails. Even if I can't respond or act on each email I categorize them by moving them to the correct folder and adding a reminder to the email for when I plan to address it further.

Many email programs offer some means of creating reminders, flags, or tasks for later work.

Scheduling

> *"Electronic calendar! - I put tasks, due dates, reminders, etc. on my calendar to stay on top of approaching needs/deadlines. Hard copy materials are organized by files, and filing system within my own office. Require staff members to also stay organized so we can step in for one another, as needed. Try to limit the [amount] of hard copy materials saved, and instead save in network files, well-organized by topic."*
>
> *- April Scrimger*

> *"A clear routine throughout the course of my day is an important ingredient. And a well maintained and an up to date calendar of events and alerts is invaluable."*
>
> *- Torin Lucas*

Planning your activities is crucial to becoming more organized. We will look at details on planning activities more in a moment. When thinking of the method of planning your time, the first major choice you have is digital planners versus paper planners. As you may have guessed based on this chapter, I recommend digital planners. At times I do find benefit to planning some things out on paper first, but ultimately it ends up in some type of digital planner, both for business and personal activities. The next sections cover some of the benefits I've seen in using digital planners over paper planners.

Ultimately, you can apply the suggestions you find here to either type of planner. Whichever you choose, just give it some thought up front. Which method offers you the best way to lay out tasks for your own personal needs?

What are some examples of digital planners, you may ask? For the office environment, Microsoft Outlook is highly recommended, especially when paired with Microsoft Exchange. Your office may already have this or another system established. Check with your manager to see what tools are already in place. For personal use I recommend Google Calendar and their other suite of free tools. These can also be used in an office setting, but check with your manager to see if it fits with your company's policies. There are other options as well, but these are two that stand out.

As promised, here are some benefits to choosing a digital planner.

Cross-Device Access

Having a paper-based planning system will definitely help get you organized. But what about portability? You can get planners which you can take with you, but that adds another thing to remember, another thing to carry.

An advantage of a digital planner is you can take it with you using devices you already own. Many popular calendar scheduling tools offer apps that run from your cell phone or tablet. This lets you view, enter, and update meetings whether you are at your work desk, home desk, or anywhere with a portable device that has internet access.

For recommended scheduling and task management applications check out www.successlifter.com/the-successful-employee.

Ease of Rescheduling

Certainly with a paper-based scheduling tool you can easily move a penciled-in appointment from one day to another when something else comes up. But what if you need to reshuffle four or five different appointments because of this one you had to move? A bit of rewriting but not too bad. Unless these appointments are meetings with other people and they need to be notified the meeting date or time has been altered.

With a digital calendar this can be much easier. Moving appointments between days is as easy as changing the date and saving the appointment. Then you can see what conflicts the move created and start adjusting other appointments without the need to re-enter any of the other associated information.

Where this really gets cumbersome with a paper-based planner is when these appointments you need to shuffle around are actually meetings with one or more people. Perhaps you need to move a meeting with three other people to the following day which causes you to have to move three other meetings you already had set. Each of the four meetings to move has multiple people attending so you need to notify each attendee of the date change and ensure they can make the meeting at its new date and time. With a paper-based planner this would involve many phone or email communications back and forth to ensure the desired attendance is possible for each meeting. With digital planners this is as simple as moving the meeting and letting the planner send emails to the participants with the new date and time for each meeting. Even better, many office environments offer digital planners which allow you to perform a busy search on other employees' calendars. This way you know if the new time is open on each of the participant's calendar before changing the date and time of the meeting. Far more efficient and productive. This frees your time for more important matters than chasing down dates for meetings.

Another disadvantage to a paper-based planner is the space limit and content restrictions.

By space limit, I'm referring to the small rectangle you have on the page that allows maybe a line or two for the appointment details. Certainly, you could get around this using a code of some type to relate to an additional sheet of paper in your planner devoted to that meeting. But this creates a manual look-up process you need to do for each meeting to get the details. With a digital calendar you can enter far more text associated to the meeting. You could even include a detailed agenda that would automatically get sent out to all meeting participants right in the appointment itself.

By content restrictions, I'm referring to the fact that the very nature of a paper-based planner restricts the contents you add for a meeting to only be static text. You cannot, for instance, attach a set of files and deliver those files to meeting participants as part of simply creating the appointment. All of this is possible with most digital planners.

Getting Your Meeting on Someone's Calendar

As mentioned earlier, with digital planners the planner automatically invites meeting attendees by email and will even automatically add the meeting to their calendar once accepted. It will also let you know if they have accepted the meeting, declined, or suggested an alternate time.

As mentioned earlier, with the busy search feature offered by many office planning tools, you can ensure the attendees' calendars are free for the desired date and time.

Organizing your digital workspace will provide you more efficiency and productivity, giving you back more precious time.

Organize Your Physical Workspace

> *"Staying organized is necessary. The easiest way for me is by making lists. Lists help me prioritize what has to be done, and also helps the employer see where I am in the process quickly. Another way I stay organized is by writing pending deadlines on the calendar. And finally, as work comes in I put the item in the corresponding files, keeping my desk clean and organized."*
>
> *- Rebecca Elliott*

> *"Writing down everything helps me stay organized. It's very easy to forget a small step. But if you write everything down, things usually run smoothly."*
>
> *- Garrick Woodberry*

Not everyone works on a computer but most jobs involve some type of physical workspace, be it a desk or a workstation of some type. Some may not even have a single location, being on the go most or all of the work day. Even someone on the go typically has some items they bring with them regularly like a briefcase or laptop bag. Being on the go, your workspace may very well be your car.

> *"I maintain a grand calendar that contains both personal and professional commitments and appointments. I prefer a neat, orderly work environment, but am notorious for having the 'filing drawer' with paper that hasn't made it to its final resting place. You can tell I'm old school - referring to paper. In the electronic world, I've struggled at keeping emails in the 'In box' under control, but have managed to develop a robust file system for electronic documents. I also use (old-school, again) a notebook for journaling meeting notes, phone conversations, project outlines, etc. on a day-by-day basis - providing a one source reference source for information and activities. When working in a traditional office I have used drive time to plan the day, understanding that in my roles, the day rarely ends up according to plan. So, the daily planning is more of a 'wish' list of things to accomplish. I also employ white boards for listing major projects and topics to make sure they are a constant visual."*
>
> *- Fran Mosher*

No matter what your physical work area is like, give some thought to how you can make that space better work for you. Look at how you can make it more efficient, more versatile, and more user-friendly.

Block thirty minutes to an hour in your day that you can devote to nothing but this single activity. You are the best person to determine how to improve your physical workspace because you know best how you use it. But you need to give your focused attention to the task of determining what will improve your workspace. Next I'll give you some areas to think through during this time. Use these thought starters to evaluate your workspace situation and apply some thoughts you have of how to improve your workspace.

Be sure you give a new idea some time to start working for you before you give up on it. Depending on the change you are making, it may take a couple weeks before you see improvement from it.

Frequently, Rarely, and Never Used Items

Are there papers, files, contact lists, etc. that you use most often? What about those you rarely or never use?

First consider each of your workspaces, if you have more than one. Think of the type of work you do in each. How often do you work in each? Have there been times over the past three months you didn't have an item with you that you needed?

If you can, get all your work items together in one place as well as any briefcases, bags, etc. you use to transport your work items. If you can't get all the items make a list of those not with you. Go through all the items. Categorize each one as to what level of interaction you have with that item on a daily, weekly, or monthly basis. Categorize the items as either frequently used, rarely used, or never used. Frequently used may be at least once a day or more than once a week. Rarely is maybe once every couple weeks or less. If you do work at multiple workspaces consider making a list for each workspace and apply this categorization for each item on each list based on how you work with the item at that location.

This may seem like a bit much, but it will give you a clear picture of how you most work with the things around you and help you make wise choices about items to keep close and items that aren't as important to keep with you all the time. Also, it will help weed out never used items that just take up space.

Once you have your list (or lists for multiple workspaces) ready, find close-at-hand locations for all your frequently used items so you can get to them right away. Then find places for your rarely used items. Your never used items may be things you don't need any more or at least not at the location you have them.

Important or Confidential Materials

Depending on the field of work you are in you may take into consideration the privacy or confidentiality level of physical documents and information. For instance, in the United States, the healthcare industry must follow strict *HIPAA (Health Insurance Portability and Accountability Act of 1996)* regulations for the proper handling of personal health information.
 - *HIPAA, U.S. Department of Health & Human Services*

The banking industry must follow the *Safeguards Rule* to ensure the confidentiality of banking members' information.
 - *Safeguards, Federal Trade Commission*

Other fields have similar governmentally mandated and enforced policies on information handling. Whatever structure you determine best for porting your documents between locations, ensure you stay in compliance with any applicable regulations. If you aren't sure, consult with your manager or security compliance department.

In my conversations with people across various industries, I have found some industries do not have governmental regulation or even a formalized, shared set of standards for how to treat and protect patron information. To me this is alarming -not so much that the government has not become involved, but rather that an organization does not place adequate protections around the information they collect and utilize. Do you work in an industry that does not have overarching regulations or standards for information handling? Do you see areas within your company that information is utilized in manners that could jeopardize the security or privacy of a customer? If the company you work for has not already enacted some policies around such information use, give some thought to what the company could do to protect this information. Try to come up with some options. Document these as best you can and bring this to your manager or enter it in the company's comment box if they have one. Even if the company is not interested in enacting such policies, are there steps you can take in your own handling of information that would protect customers? These steps should fit into your current workflow and not cause limitations to your ability to perform your duties.

If there are currently no agreed standards or government oversight and you see issues with potential information compromise, it is very possible regulations may be invoked at some point in the future - if not by your company then perhaps by the government. Being ready ahead of time could save you rushed work to implement a solution once it is enforced and potentially save your company money.

Hand-Off

Planning a vacation soon? Are there processes someone will need to take over for you? Do you find yourself providing the same walk-through or instructions you did last time you went on vacation? Perhaps the one taking on the process for you forgot how to perform the operation since it has been a while. Or maybe the one taking the process hasn't done it before.

What can you do to prevent this re-teaching of your process? Documentation. Take some time to think through all your processes that could be done by someone else in your absence. Document the steps. Maybe the process seems easy to you after having done it many times, but to someone new to the process it may not seem as elementary. Reference documentation can prove invaluable to the one taking on your process - a safety net of sorts.

Be sure to include in the documentation a section for troubleshooting. If you know of some common mistakes you make, or someone unfamiliar with the process may make, document those. Include details on how to avoid them and how to correct them should they occur.

This could provide you some real benefits during your vacation. Peace of mind. Knowing your processes are being done, and in the fashion you would if you were there. Freedom. Have you ever been called during your vacation to answer questions on a process you normally perform? Did you have to step away from your family or friends to walk someone through the process? Was it a process that could have been documented ahead of time?

A vacation is planned so you typically have some degree of time to hand some things off to others. However, something unplanned could be disastrous without something which can be provided to others in your absence. If you have an unexpected sick day that turns into a few more. If you have an unexpected family emergency. Do you know if you had to quickly step away that your processes would be taken care of?

Some may find a sense of job security in being the only one at the company who knows how to do a set of processes. The thought of documenting these may make such a person feel they are now expendable; no longer of value to the company as anyone could now perform these processes with them being so well documented. Certainly concern over one's job security is a valid and warranted consideration. Valuing your employment, you would not want to do things which jeopardize your employment status. But is this really one of them?

Naturally all employers and managers are different in the manner in which they would respond to different workplace situations so everyone's experience may not be the same. As with all suggestions and recommendations throughout this book, consider how they would fit within your current organization. Take what advice works; tweak it to fit your situation.

EXERCISE

Now let's consider some possible perspectives as a manager. How might a manager (specifically your manager) react to the following two hypothetical situations?

Situation 1: Robert enjoys his job greatly and would not wish to risk becoming unneeded by his company. Many come to him for specific questions about the systems he works knowing if anyone would have the answer about the system it would be Robert. In fact, he prides himself on being so well versed in his applications and the only one at the company that knows how to do most any of the maintenance involved with these systems. Robert decides to take a week of much needed vacation. Unfortunately, while he is away he finds he is continually on his cell phone answering questions just as if he was in the office. He usually enjoys being needed, but now he starts to feel unable to get the elusive downtime he so desired from this vacation. To make matters worse, when he returns to the office he finds out about several key processes he would normally take care of that he forgot to remotely connect to his computer and perform while on vacation. After all, he is the only one that can run these processes and he doesn't want anyone taking them from him. Arriving to his desk he sees a note from his boss to come see him and discuss the ramifications of these processes having been neglected.

<u>Write in your notebook</u>:

What is Robert's manager probably going to talk to him about?

Will Robert receive any positive or negative consequences in some fashion?

Has Robert put his manager in a good or bad position with his boss and others in the company?

Certainly Robert's boss may have some ownership here for not identifying the issue created by the siloed information Robert is in charge of. But was there more Robert could have done without risking his employment?

Now let's look at another possibility.

Situation 2: Similar to Robert, Marlene enjoys her work and does not wish to risk her employment with the company. In fact, she often works with her manager and others in the organization to find ways to improve existing processes. She schedules thirty to sixty minutes every month to review her current processes to ensure everything she does is properly documented and repeatable by others in the organization. These documents are shared within her team and with her manager to ensure smooth transition of processes between team members when needed, be that for workload rebalancing, out of office coverage, or introduction of new processes. Marlene is planning to be out of office to visit out-of-state family for a week so she makes sure all her processes are up to date. This takes very little time considering her regular documentation maintenance. While visiting family, she is able to focus on enjoying quality time with them, not having received any calls from work. While away Marlene's processes were all completed by her team with little to no issue and no need to reach out to her. Once she returns to

> her desk she sees a note on her desk from her boss asking to see her to discuss the process documentation standards she introduced into the office.
>
> <u>Write in your notebook</u>:
>
> What is Marlene's manager probably going to talk to her about?
>
> Will Marlene receive any positive or negative feedback or actions in some fashion?
>
> Has Marlene put her manager in a good or bad position with her boss and others in the company?

These cases are rather extreme to show their contrast and can hardly reflect all possible outcomes and reactions. A main takeaway I hope is evident from these situations is that sharing what we know with others within the company builds the company's ability to function smoothly. It benefits the company and a manager should recognize and respect that from his or her employees. If a manager instead views employees as expendable based on such shared information, a valuable set of skills is being underutilized within that team.

Portability

If you work in different locations or take work home from time to time, is there a place you can designate for portable materials? Keeping them in your briefcase, for instance, so they are with you at each location?

If you do utilize a computer, tablet, or cell phone as part of your daily work, you may consider converting paper documents you need with you at different locations into electronic documents you can access from a laptop, desktop computer, tablet, or cell phone as needed. Now there are some considerations here. Consider the security level of the document and decide if a portable or electronic placement of the document meets your company's security policies. If you are ever in doubt check with your manager or the team in charge of security. They should be able to recommend and configure a secure out-of-office solution such as a Virtual Private Network (VPN). A VPN simply allows you to make a special, secure connection that allows an electronic device used outside of your work facility to act as though you are sitting right at your desk in the office. Your company's security team can provide more detail on how to get started if this is allowed at your organization.

Getting organized is something we can't consider a "someday" luxury in today's fast-paced world. For better or worse we live in the information age and probably the greatest responsibility we have for working with the multitudes of information is how to keep productive in the ever-growing wealth of information. Organizing a structured, clean, and efficient work environment will allow you to handle greater amounts of information and give you a competitive edge over others in the workplace.

Detail Oriented

To start moving in a direction is an important first step. Refinement comes later. But many times details are essential to making the best, most effective first impression possible.

Do people really pay attention to details? Does anyone really consider the specifics when the general structure seems intact?

You bet they do. Have you ever read a book and spotted a glaring grammatical error? Sure you knew what the author meant to say, but did it affect your view of that author in a negative way at all? What if it wasn't just one grammatical error but ten or more? Just details, right? I mean, if you get the general idea it is enough, isn't it?

That doesn't seem to be the case from my experience. Even if you are never called out on these details that slip by, they do make an impression. But you may say these are just mistakes and we all make mistakes. That is very true. We all do make mistakes. But at the same time there are methods we can take to reduce and try to even eliminate these mistakes or missed details. Perhaps we can't eliminate them all on our first pass at creating something, but review and editing can polish a finished work.

As you think through your next project and plan out how to tackle the requirements, go back through your solution. Are you missing any details you should be accounting for? Is there anything you can catch now before someone else does - a manager, or even worse, a customer?

Next time you are at work in the factory, are there steps you will skip because they really don't seem important? Are there steps to your work process that could create a defect or risk to the end user? These are all areas to consider.

Is it really your job to think about these things? Is this just for the manager of your department or the quality control team to worry about? That may be true. Your role at the company might not include this type of evaluation. But isn't this also a good opportunity to improve your standing as an employee within your organization? Not to mention the potential positive outcome of preventing the next big safety recall that could seriously injure a consumer. That may not be the case with what you find, but if you have the mindset of evaluating processes around you, you will be more likely to recognize the big oversights no one else has seen yet.

In this chapter on getting and staying organized we presented many ideas you can try. These can represent some major changes. You may not want to try implementing them all at once. Maybe just one or two to start with. Then when you feel comfortable and have those integrated, try another couple.

How you implement these methods may take some thought. Everyone's situation is unique. Explore some ideas on how these methods could be implemented. Don't be discouraged if something doesn't work. If you implement your ideas and you see no real improvement even after giving it adequate time, don't be frustrated. Anytime we try something worthwhile we will have ideas that don't produce the results we want. Not every idea works out to produce the desired results no matter how great it seems when you had the idea. The important thing here is to not get discouraged. Often it takes working through ideas that don't work to reach those that do.

7. GOALS MANAGEMENT

> *"Early in my career I learned that if I could become an 'expert' at something, doors opened and I was given more responsibility. This meant pursuing knowledge outside of the workplace. I also learned that being a good conversationalist provided opportunity to talk with people at all levels, giving the impression of being one who sees the big picture. Being a better employee also meant doing menial tasks - sending the message that the good of the company took precedence over personal status."*
>
> *- Fran Mosher*

At the beginning of the book I had you take some time to think about and even define what success means to you. As mentioned, success can mean something very different to different people. Now let's build on that. Defining the picture of what success means for you is a vision. Something you want to achieve at some point during this journey. But it is just that - a journey. And journeys have transition points along the way.

If you want to take a vacation to the Bahamas, there are several transition points. Ultimately, your vision is seeing yourself relaxing on the beach in the Bahamas soaking up the warm sun. That's great! But how do you get there? You plan out each step of what it takes to get there. You may even have to make some adjustments along the way, reevaluating and improving the map. You plan to drive your car to the airport, making sure to leave extra time for traffic. On the way there's construction causing you to reroute. You get to the airport and your flight is delayed by 20 minutes. Unscathed by the delay, you pull out that novel you brought along just for such an occasion.

I think you get the idea. It isn't as simple as saying you will walk out your front door and end up in the Bahamas. It is up to you to chart the course to reach your destination. There are plenty of resources along the way to help you get there, but ultimately the path you choose is yours.

Making the vision of relaxing on the Bahama beach a reality is precisely the way to approach making the vision of becoming a successful employee become a reality. Well, okay, not precisely the same path, but certainly the same approach of breaking the journey up into segments.

So what are these segments I'm talking about? Goals. Long-term goals. Short-term goals. Goals are the drivers, the stepping stones that help you advance in your path until you reach the ultimate goal and realize the vision.

The most effective way to make that happen is to start with a clearly defined vision of what being a successful employee means to you. Then look at where you are right now. Keep a clear image of the vision in your mind as you think about what steps you can take over the next week, the next month, the next quarter, to move even just a little closer to that vision.

The pace you set for this advance is up to you, but be realistic as to what you can accomplish in a short term. Also push yourself some so as to not become idle in your progress.

Maybe you can start with the recommendations on becoming more organized that were described earlier. If this seems an overwhelming task, don't give up on it. That is just a sign the goal is too big and needs to be broken down into some smaller goals.

Goals can build on each other (and often do) to reach another goal. Set up some short-term goals you can knock out in a matter of days that make a bigger goal more approachable.

Document Your Goals

Thinking through these goals is great, but it is hard to build an action plan against them and execute against that plan if it is all just in your head. Document the goals you are defining. This can be electronic or on paper; whichever works best for you. But do document them. This provides accountability and a means to measure your forward progress as well.

A goal has to be tangible. It has to be measurable. It has to be something you can say without a doubt that you have either reached it or you have not. When you define a goal and document it, make sure you will be able to know when it is complete. For instance, "Help others better know my processes in case they have to cover for me when I'm out" is a somewhat vague goal. When do you plan to achieve this goal? How do you know this has been completed? Here is a goal that is easy to measure and determine if and when it is completed: "Create process documentation for three of my processes by the end of this month." The second goal doesn't fully complete all your processes but it is a stepping stone that you can build on and draw momentum from. Plus, you can start implementing the solution as you go, so by the end of the month you can already be offering your coworkers documentation on some key processes.

Build Tasks Toward Your Goals

Tasks can break down a goal even further. This helps you see even more progress on a daily basis as you advance on your goals. Let's start with the goal we defined earlier: "Create process documentation for three of my processes by the end of this month." Three starter tasks you might create under this goal could be:

1. Use the template provided in the bonus material for this book. (You can find the document and bonus material at www.successlifter.com/the-successful-employee. Feel free to use it as is or modify it for your purposes.)

2. Fill out the process document for one of your processes.

3. Share the process just documented with two co-workers and ask them to comment if this is helpful and how it could be improved to give them the information needed.

Just like with your goal, attach a due date to each of these tasks.

EXERCISE

Using your notebook, write down three projects.

For each of these projects list out two or three goals.

Under each goal write out four or five tasks.

Plan Each Week Based on Tasks and Goals

Once a week, plan what your upcoming week looks like. This shouldn't take too long as most of the work was already done building out your goals and tasks earlier. Look at your task and goal due dates and determine what fits for this week. Make adjustments as needed based on what else needs to fit into your week.

If you find your dates are slipping often, or you have trouble sticking to the dates you set and keep changing them, you may just need some accountability. Find someone else you work with interested in also improving their role as an employee. They can be on your team or another team. Start following and posting on topics at www.successlifter.com. This site was created to help you achieve your unique vision of success!

If you can't find someone wanting to work through a plan such as this with you, see if you can just find someone that is willing to keep you accountable on your dates. Provide them your task and goal due dates and ask that they check in with you weekly to ensure you are on track. Ask them to always ask you for a good reason why a date had to be pushed out. You don't need to offer them all the details of the task or goal if you would rather not. Even just the due date for each of them and some way to reference them is enough.

Having accountability from someone else can be that extra push to drive you forward.

8. RELATE WELL TO OTHERS

"Try not to be judgmental. Be kind, courteous and respectful. Offer to help when needed and be encouraging to them."
- Ellen Coppler

Team Oriented

"For me, I found that showing interest in different projects helps the employer to see I am wanting to participate in making their business the best it could be. Another way I found is by being organized. Being organized makes the tasks given to me run smoothly making it easier for me to reach task deadlines and saving the employer money. And finally, communication. Speaking with others in the company, knowing what happens between departments helps me make their jobs easier as well as vice versa. I think keeping lines of communication open helps the company find and solve problems faster."
- Rebecca Elliott

> *"Watch and listen to the 'better employee.' If there is not a "better employee" you need to find some sort of inspiration. Once you get inspired get others inspired around you so you can push off one another. I find it's easier to be better as a group, hold each other accountable and give each other a little competitive feeling. When you have peers you can talk about being better which always inspired me to go practice being better. Resources are all around us but I find my biggest resource is the community I am in."*
> *- Michael Grenzicki*

Different jobs can call for different types of work. Even different projects. Working by yourself or working in a group. The dynamics of working in a group, or team, is somewhat different than working individually. For some jobs you may be relatively autonomous and able to complete all your tasks without relying on anyone else for their work. If you work on a factory line, for instance, you may feel your job is self-contained. You have control over your part from start to finish, having no reliance on anyone else. Is this entirely the case? What if the parts you assemble are provided by the assembly of others within the company? What if they are falling behind in production? Will your output be reduced?

Many jobs require some type of interaction. It might be with other team members or with someone from a different department within the organization. All the workers within the company are on the same team - the team that helps drive the company forward. This creates an interdependence between workers at the same company even if you don't regularly interact with them.

So why is all this important? How you interact with others within your company can affect the difficulty level and reward level you experience from your job.

Let's look at the factory line example again. Let's say Josh is working the factory line that gets parts from another line. Amanda works the line that provides products to Josh's line. Josh has never interacted with Amanda. However, he has had plenty opportunity to interact with her arriving to and departing work. Even lunch breaks provided ample time. Josh really just wanted to come to work, do his job, then go home. There is really nothing wrong with that. But since Amanda doesn't know Josh she may not see her productivity slowdown as affecting Josh. She just sees it as setting back the production line a little - a more abstract impact than a personal one.

Josh's difficulty level just went up and his feeling of reward from his job may have gone down as his productivity numbers are impacted.

> *"Peer pressure is a powerful force. Particularly if you're working with people whom you respect and don't want to let down, the motivation to help your team succeed can override the dips in motivation that you encounter on days when you're not at your best."*
>
> *- Quora, Forbes*

What if instead Josh had built a rapport with Amanda? Amanda may then want to ensure her line is up as best as she can, knowing it would impact Josh if she fell behind.

Obviously, Amanda has an obligation to the company with or without considering any impact to Josh. This alone should be enough motivation. But, there is something to be said about the personal element of working with people and not just for things.

> *"There are challenges each day in any workplace, and a strong team environment can act as a support mechanism for staff members. Work group members can help each other improve their performance and work together toward improving their professional development. Team members also come to rely on each other and trust each other. These bonds can be important when the team faces a particularly difficult challenge or if the group is forced to deal with the loss of a team member while still trying to maintain productivity."*
>
> *- George N. Root III*

Some jobs or projects require you to work with a team of other peers. These teams can be from the same department or even different departments. Each person in the team has a role to play. It can be easy to adopt the mindset that once you know your task, you just need to focus on that task alone and the rest of the team just needs to work on their tasks. And to some degree this is what happens. However, maintaining the team connectivity is needed. Projects seldom go exactly as planned from the onset. So, midway in the project you may see some shifts in priorities or order in which things are done. Team members may need to adjust their own planned workflow for the good of the overall team and project's success.

Contribute in Meetings

Meetings can be intimidating, especially for someone just starting out. Even if you have been working for many years, meetings can become time consuming and even feel like an interruption to your daily work. I have heard many complain about such meetings and, I admit, I myself have too. Below we will look at a few things that can help this perspective. If you are new to the workforce and feel intimidated by meetings, this will help offer you a better understanding of the purpose and objective so you can better find your fit in the meeting. If you have been at this for a while but feel discouraged by the time these meetings take away from completing your work, this will shine light on the underlying benefit these meetings provide.

Is this your first time attending business meetings? Have you attended several already but still feel intimidated by the structure or expectations of the meeting? Before going into the meeting, prepare yourself. Being prepared for a meeting can make you feel more like a vital contributor to the meeting, thus helping to offset any fears you have. If you don't know the purpose of the meeting approach the person that invited you or your manager and ask what the goal of the meeting is. Then think about why your presence is required in the meeting. What is expected of you? Is there something you need to prepare ahead of time that you will be asked to speak to during the meeting?

If you have access to the room you will be meeting in, check it out prior to the meeting. Think about where you might be sitting. Who else will be attending the meeting and what do you expect they will be contributing?

Getting familiar with the space and context of the meeting can help calm your nerves. Preparing materials and information ahead of time will also serve to keep you from becoming anxious. You may be asked something unexpected during the meeting, but the more prepared you are the better equipped you will be to handle any questions that do come up.

From time to time I receive meeting invites with little to no description as to the nature of the meeting. If you are invited to such a meeting, don't be afraid to check with the meeting organizer or some of the other participants for more information regarding the meeting topic.

Some meetings may feel like the information is not that helpful for you or doesn't pertain to you. It can be easy to dwell on work you could be accomplishing rather than focusing on the meeting. Instead of giving in to that temptation, try finding a way to make this meeting productive. Everyone has a unique viewpoint. As you hear and try to better understand the topics being discussed think about what considerations have not yet been mentioned. If you think of something new, offer it up. You were invited to the meeting for a reason and even if it wasn't for the current topic discussed, your suggestions may be helpful to others in the meeting. Be sure that you are presenting your thoughts in a respectful method, taking into consideration the group of people in the meeting, and the management structure in place.

If you feel you will be viewed as out of place by offering your suggestion, try conveying this to your manager if he or she is present, or ask your manager later for the best course of presenting your ideas.

You never know where your suggestions could lead or what improvements they could foster within your organization.

Dress for the Job Wanted

> *"Dressing for success seems to be an old adage, but it still holds true. Very successful employees typically set the standard for others."*
>
> *- Fran Mosher*

Earlier in this book we talked about dressing appropriately for work. Now let's look at a step beyond that. More than just dressing in an acceptable manner, it is good to dress for the job you are hoping to get.

Hoping to land that supervisor position? Wanting to advance into management?

Dressing for the job you want can be one way to get others thinking about the possibility of you in that role. Sure there are other more direct things to be doing to let others know you are looking to advance and we are covering many of those here too. But this is another way to bolster that message to management.

Just like our body language, grooming choices, and other social queues, the way we dress sends specific, unspoken messages to those around us about how we want them to perceive us. This is yet another area you can choose to take control of and create the perception you desire rather than leave that perception entirely to chance.

Use your best judgment on if or how to apply this suggestion of dressing for the job you want. Some jobs it won't make sense to do this. Some jobs you can't do this, as the job may require a specific uniform or type of attire that would prevent you from dressing as you would for the job you hope to acquire. Decide if this is a good fit for your current position and to what degree.

Get to Know Those Higher in the Company

Some companies present an almost military-like command hierarchy. There are certainly advantages to this approach for maintaining order, accountability, and a solid chain of command. However, it may leave you feeling unable to get to know those higher up in the company.

Fortunately, at least for the thoughts of corporate advancement, not all companies are quite so rigidly structured. There is usually some type of chain of command which you need to utilize accordingly and in compliance with company policy. Yet, getting your name and face in front of some higher up in the company may help if your goal is to step into a management role in the future at that company.

I am by no means suggesting skirting company policy or going around your manager. This can be as simple as saying, "Good morning Mr. Smith" to the CEO when you next see him in the hallway. Depending on how approachable upper management is within your company, this may even take the form of sending an email to the CTO asking about the company's recent decision to buy XYZ Company. Express your interest to know if your department may be given projects along with XYZ Company employees. Now this request is likely one best brought forward through your manager but, again, you need to be aware of the company's unique structure before considering this type of approach.

Work Well With, and Anticipate The Needs of, Your Customer

In one fashion or another you have a customer. You may be quick to refute this statement. But even if you don't directly work with a customer of the company, at the very least your customer is the company itself - likely more specific individuals or teams within the company more than the entire company as a whole.

Give that statement some thought. Very specifically try to identify who your customers are at the company you work for. This helps you properly align your priorities as your customers are a very important aspect of what you do.

Once you have these customers identified, think about each one as they are all different and will all interact with you differently. What ways do you serve your customer well right now? What needs does your customer have that are either currently unmet or not fully met by you? How could you better meet those needs? If you aren't sure, ask! You may not want to make this an open invitation to assign you mountains of work, but tailor your questions to narrow in on one or two areas you could serve your customer better. Build a plan to meet those needs and start doing just that.

Then watch the impact it has on your customer. Will your proactive initiative show your customer you mean business when you want to help them? Certainly.

Now one fear you may have here is if you start exploring new opportunities to help your customer, you will quickly be given far more work than you can do.

Don't be afraid to prioritize your work efforts. Some of these new things can happen, but maybe just not right now. If your customers start wanting things sooner, this is an excellent way to show your manager that business is growing and in need of additional staff.

Before jumping in and offering extensive new services to customers it is advisable to sit down with your manager. Make sure he or she knows your current workload and any need for additional help. These new opportunities may even result in additional payment from your customers for the new work, resulting in new money for your company.

Give Full Attention in Conversations

> *"I try to relate to others by showing interest in their lives. It might be as easy as sharing a similar interest, such as a hobby or a TV show. I also ask for assistance when I need it, I think this shows that we all need help at times and I appreciate their thoughts. And I try to answer questions/or solve problems if asked."*
>
> *- Rebecca Elliott*

> *"I usually start with trying to listen and understand where the other person is coming from. I always [try] to be supportive and positive in my responses and discussion with peers at the workplace."*
>
> *- Julie Bolinger*

Have you ever wanted to share an important event with a friend and they just didn't seem all that interested in hearing you? Too busy or preoccupied to hear you? Maybe you could tell they were thinking about what they wanted to say, just waiting for a pause in your words long enough that they could start talking about what was on their mind.

How does an experience like that leave you feeling? Rejected, misunderstood, unimportant? Not good outcomes for a personal conversation. Not good outcomes for a business conversation either.

> *"Be approachable and friendly. Seek to understand their perspective and goal. Do not put focus on positional hierarchy - we all have a purpose or we wouldn't be doing our given job."*
> *- April Scrimger*

When relating to others at work we should make an effort to actively listen. be that in a conversation with managers over you, employees under you, or coworkers. In business conversation or when socializing with coworkers, try to create a better outcome for the conversation by being an active listener. Providing others an attentive, listening ear will make them far more likely to offer you the same.

So how do we do this? How do we ensure we are actively listening?

The first thing you can do right away to improve conversation is maintain eye contact. That doesn't mean you have to keep your eyes fixed on the other person's eyes the entire time, but avoid looking around the room or down, especially while the other person is talking to you.

Keep your mind engaged. Sometimes our minds will wander while listening to someone speak. It can take some conscious effort to gently bring your thoughts back to the conversation so you don't miss what is being said.

> *"By listening, I find common areas of interest. If there are none I inquire more about their interests and share mine."*
> *- Ernest Randall Taylor*

Give the person time to think and articulate their thoughts. Some of us speak quickly while others give extra thought to each word and phrase. If you think and speak quickly, you may feel a desire to draw the thoughts out of your friend or coworker. This is when you need to relax a bit and give the person speaking time to express their words in the manner they need to.

Be aware of body language. Observe gestures, postures, inflections, and facial expressions to better understand the words.

Use questions that encourage the speaker to express thoughts in his or her own manner rather than questions that try to force a response. Perhaps a question like, "What happened next?" instead of "A better way to handle that would have been ____. Why didn't you do that?"

Being an active listener demonstrates to others you are ready and willing to hear them. Knowing how to listen can be a valuable asset in making you a better employee.

The Successful Employee

"I have employed a 'walk around' approach to organizations, checking in on other departments as a way of demonstrating interest and learning about the problems of others. A technique for which I have been very lax is having lunch in the breakroom or cafeteria, when the opportunity to form relationships is very strong and in an informal setting. Unfortunately, I have often opted to eat in my office, using the time for reading or personal activities. (I recommend this, but am not the role model for the effort.) Being well read on a variety of topics has also been important to relating to others. Of course, asking more questions, and revealing self on a personal level has always served to seal relationships."

- Fran Mosher

"One thing I've found that I think is important is to talk to coworkers socially. In my career, I am able to have lunch with a small group of coworkers. It is also quite common for colleagues to stay after work and have conversations to wind down, share ideas, or just catch up with each other. It's also important to participate in some of the "fun" parts of staff meetings - celebrate birthdays, weddings, babies, retirements."

- Bradlee Clegg

Handle Stress

Handling stress can be a challenge. As much as possible, stay calm and collected when stress comes. Does this mean you should never feel stress? Certainly not. At one point or another you will probably experience stress in your career.

A project the boss just told you is due a week earlier. You get asked to work late, already having worked a full day and ready for a break. The product launch was going great until a key teammate had an unexpected leave of absence. These are just a few examples of things in the workplace that can cause stress.

Before we go into how to handle stress at work, let's define some signs of stress to watch for. Fatigue, muscle tension, headaches, sleeping difficulties, and stomach upset are some possible symptoms. Anxiety, discouragement, feeling overwhelmed, trouble concentrating, aggression, mood swings, and becoming easily frustrated are also likely indicators of stress. If you feel one or more of these symptoms, it does not necessarily mean you are experiencing stress, but these are certainly things to consider.

Stress has come to mean something negative and avoided at all cost. Yet, some stress can actually be helpful. A due date for a project that is just enough of a push to give you the motivation needed to get the job done. Knowing the unfavorable outcome of a job not done to the best of your abilities. These are just two examples of how a stress can actually help you in reaching your goals. The favorable stressors in these examples are 'the due date' and 'the risk of an unfavorable outcome.'

It isn't really stress we should be concerned about so

much as overstress. When stress reaches a point greater than we can manage, we begin feeling overstress.

So, now that you know some of the things to watch for, what do you do you when overstress comes? Here are some tips to help with that.

Calm and center your thoughts.

Relax. Your thoughts racing from one responsibility to the next can quickly increase your stress. While we mentioned some stress is good, too much can have harmful effects physically as well as mentally.

Once you feel your mind racing and you start feeling signs of stress, find a way to regain control of your thoughts. If you are able, step away from the problem. Physically that is. Change location to someplace you can recenter your thoughts. If you aren't able to physically step away, try to mentally distance yourself from the problem for a moment. Put things into perspective. Remind yourself the condition you are in will only serve to worsen the situation. You need to relax and get a clear head to be able to work out a good plan.

A few deep, slow, calming breaths can quickly reduce your heart rate and help you feel in control of your own thoughts again.

The Healthwise staff at WebMD explain different breathing methods including the 4-7-8 breathing method. Here is how to try the method:

1. To start, put one hand on your belly and the other on your chest.

2. Take a deep, slow breath from your belly, and silently count to 4 as you breathe in.

3. Hold your breath, and silently count from 1 to 7.

4. Breathe out completely as you silently count from 1 to 8. Try to get all the air out of your lungs by the time you count to 8.

5. Repeat 3 to 7 times or until you feel calm.

6. Notice how you feel at the end of the exercise.

- Healthwise, WebMD

Identify the cause.

Why did stress become overstress? Where is it coming from? Is it a single source or multiple sources? Once you know what is creating the overstress, you can start thinking about how to combat it.

Make it smaller.

When stress turns to overstress it may involve one or both of these feelings: "I don't have what it takes (or know what it takes) to do this," and, "I can do this but there is just too much." The cause of your stress may be more complex than just one thing. There may be several parts that are creating excessive stress. Each of those parts may fit into one or the other of the above statements.

Once you have identified the cause of your overstress, break it down into smaller pieces. Certainly, you need to deal with the entire collection of stressors but likely not all at the same time. That feeling of needing to do it all at once is a large cause of overstress. The myth of multitasking has created an illusion that to be successful we must do more than one thing at a time. The reality is more of a strategic shifting between responsibilities. Think of the image of the circus performer spinning multiple plates, each plate on its own stick. How does he keep them all going at the same time with just his two hands? The trick is, he doesn't. He strategically shifts his time and attention from one plate to the next. He doesn't just pick any plate - he picks the one that is most critical, needing attention the most. Once he has stabilized that plate he moves on to the next and so on.

This example of the plate spinning circus performer provides a starting point for dealing with stress, but the goal is not to stay in that cycle long term. This approach is to get us back to a more sustainable model while mitigating as much damage as possible during the crisis.

Break the stressors down into as small of pieces as make sense. Then decide what the stress is from each piece. Is it not knowing what to do with it or just that there are too many altogether? For those you aren't sure what to do with, try to find someone with the answers you need or that can help you resolve that piece. For the others, make a plan of how to prioritize them and start attacking them one at a time. As you work each one, try to avoid dwelling on how many are left. Trust the plan you have mapped out and focus on the task at hand.

Have you ever seen a horse carriage ride and wondered about the headgear they have the horses wear? You may notice a square, black section protruding from the headgear next to each eye of the horse. These are blinders. They don't blind all the horse's vision, just side and back. This keeps the horse focused on the task of moving forward. The carriage driver keeps alert of what is happening around and behind the horses and corrects the horse's path accordingly.

The plan of attack you made is much like the carriage driver. The plan has taken into account priorities and set a course for how to get to a favorable outcome. Once you start working through the map you set out, you put blinders on so to speak. If changes come that impact your map you will want to watch for those, but the idea of the blinders is to keep you from re-thinking your map out of anxiety. You have spent the time to establish the best map you could; now is the time to forge ahead piece by piece.

Seek life balance.

Over the years I have found many aspects of life thrive within a balance. Too much of one end of a spectrum or the other can drain the joy from an endeavor. What do I mean by this? Your work life and your personal and family life can be thought of as two ends of a spectrum. Too much work and you may start getting overstressed by things that normally you would not. The joy can be pulled out of what you do at work leaving you feeling unsatisfied in your personal and family life as well.

I'm sure I'm not the only one that has experienced a day that I wish I could just not work at all. I mean, if this is causing me so much difficulty in my life, why should I be doing this at all? Many hope for just that. Perhaps by winning the lottery I'll never have to work again. But would this fix the problem? The work you do can provide an anchor in your life. A mission of sorts. Certainly our purpose in life is made up of far more than our occupation, but our job does provide us something to stretch ourselves for. Something to get better for. A reason to strive and try and reach and succeed. Would we still have that without work?

This is a common problem with some who enter retirement, suddenly leaving the work they had known for so much of their life. Some even feel a sense of no longer belonging and even like they have lost purpose.

Rosa says, *"I am recently retired and like many longed for leisure time, time to meditate on life and to do things I had always wanted to do."* She goes on to explain:

> *"I am still in contact with my place of employment, where I had a very successful career, but had to retire at a specified age, although my projects were not completed. Due to cut backs and the current economic situation, the person I had expected to replace me could not be hired and thus everything I created is slowly falling into decay. So I find myself depressed and without purpose."*
>
> *- Rosa*

Finding the right balances in life can provide us an environment of creativity, fulfillment, and joy.

<u>Exercise, eat well, and rest</u>.

It can be hard to make time for exercise. Sticking to a structured eating plan can be challenging. Getting enough sleep at night can be hard with so many things vying for your time.

Yes, it is hard to maintain a healthy lifestyle. How to do so is beyond the scope of this particular book, so I have compiled a list of resources to help you in this area. Check them out at www.successlifter.com/the-successful-employee. Keeping your body at its peak will help you cope with stress far better than you would otherwise.

> *"Exercise is also considered vital for maintaining mental fitness, and it can reduce stress. Studies show that it is very effective at reducing fatigue, improving alertness and concentration, and at enhancing overall cognitive function. This can be especially helpful when stress has depleted your energy or ability to concentrate.*
>
> *When stress affects the brain, with its many nerve connections, the rest of the body feels the impact as well. Or, if your body feels better, so does your mind."*
>
> *- Michael Otto*

If you aren't sure the best exercise and diet, you should consult your primary care physician for sound medical advice before starting.

Look for Ways to Help and Promote Others

> *"In the words of my grandchildren, 'Packing a smile' is always a winning effort in the employee game. Invest in others and success will come your way. Seek out those who are struggling and offer your mentorship and friendship. Look for ways to 'cover' your supervisor's back - (s)he needs your support more than they will admit. Keep your language clean and edifying."*
>
> *- Fran Mosher*

> *"Generally, just be willing to help people. This can leave a good impression on them as well as your managers. Don't lose sight of the fact that you all work on a team, you succeed and fail together. Focus on self and team improvement, the rewards might not be just monetary. You might find lifelong friends along the way by simply being an active listener, open to change, and willing to tackle hard or unknown problems."*
>
> *- C.J. Gonzalez*

Watch out for number one. Is that a phrase you have heard before? Is it a motto you have followed in your career? Often the world drills this point into us. Who else is going to take care of you, right? I think this view is changing and really has changed. Companies are latching on to the idea of paying it forward - a concept of offering acts of kindness to their employees and the culture at large. Certainly there may be a motivation to cast a favorable light on the company and boost employee morale. Some companies come up with some great ways to do that which truly do benefit employees and culture.

TripAdvisor is a company that helps you with planning your vacation and finding good rates on places to stay. TripAdvisor offers something special to its employees as well.

> *"Lunch is provided three times a week at TripAdvisor's office and each week, staff donate what they would've spent on food to charities that are selected by employees themselves."*
> *- Kimberly Williams*

Amazon started as an online book retailer then expanded over the past several years into selling various types of products. Among many other perks, Amazon provides its employees ownership in the company itself. From Amazon's website regarding employee benefits:

> *"We want Amazon employees to think like owners, and awarding equity provides an ownership opportunity to employees. Therefore, eligible employees receive Restricted Stock Units (RSUs) from Amazon.com Inc. as part of our global compensation model. All Amazon employees participate directly in the success of the entire company."*
> *- Amazon Benefits*

It isn't just companies that can, and I think should, adopt this type of pay it forward mentality. Each one of us has numerous ways we can apply that same principle, in little ways and not so little ways. Here are just a few ideas to get you thinking:

- When you share an insight you learned from a coworker with your boss and he congratulates you for it, give your coworker credit.
- Know the strengths of your coworkers. Be willing to suggest opportunities you come across within the company that may be a good fit for them.

Don't Say "Yes" Just to Please the Boss

Have you ever had your boss ask you to do something and you said yes only to realize later that the request is not possible or required more effort than your boss realized? It can be hard to say no at times. Especially to your boss.

> *"Often times, our guilt, fear and anxiety rule our minds when we say no."*
> *- Savannah Marie*

Does saying no seem selfish? Do you feel others will think you are unwilling to help? Certainly you want to be willing to help others. Saying no to everyone is not the best approach either. But sometimes accommodating a request in exactly the form or timing it was asked for can turn out to not be what was best for that person, company, or possibly you. It is okay to take time to think about your response.

Years ago, when I first started interviewing for jobs, I thought my answers to interview questions had to be quick. I felt if I was not responsive enough my interviewer would think I don't know what I'm talking about. This was not the case at all. An interview is more like a conversation. If you are asked a complex question and give a very quick answer that could show you really didn't think about what you said. It is okay to think through your answers. Give it some thought before you speak. In an interview you can only stretch the time out so far before you need to give an answer. However, if someone approaches you at your desk or station don't be afraid to say you need some time to think about the request so you can better understand the situation and what you can best offer.

Another consideration is importance versus urgency. Is the request you've been given an immediate need? Will it take a great deal of time to shift your thinking away from your current work, then back later? Will you lose your spot or will it take a while to get your head back into what you are working on? These are all considerations to ask yourself and possibly even the person making a request of you. Sometimes the request can wait a little while.

> *"Most questions or favors asked of you do not require immediate attention. If they do, see if the timing is appropriate for you and determine if you need to be directly involved. It's okay to tell your friend or colleague that you need some time to think about it. You'll grant yourself the chance to step away from the immediacy and pressure and have time to evaluate the pros and cons of your decision."*
> *- Savannah Marie*

9. EXPAND YOUR DOMAIN

"Always aim to exceed expectations."
- Ernest Randall Taylor

Lead

Leadership is something only someone with a title of manager or higher needs to be thinking of, right? Not so much. While the art of leadership is very important to learn and cultivate as a manager, leadership isn't just about shepherding employees under you.

There are many ways people have defined what leadership means. A good working definition for what I'm getting at in this section is this:

> *"Leadership is the capacity to translate vision into reality."*
> *- Warren Bennis*

What vision do you have? Your vision to become a more successful employee can be inspiration to others.

Inspiration as they watch you turn that vision into reality in your career. In effect, leading those around you possibly into similar habits of improvement.

Do you have a coworker that is fairly new to the job? Someone that could benefit from your coming alongside them? This is a leadership opportunity. Even if your boss hasn't specifically asked it of you, looking for ways to help this new employee will be beneficial for you both, and ultimately for your boss and the company. The benefit to the employee is a quicker, less stressful ramp-up time learning a new job. This is also a benefit to your boss and the company as it saves them time and money getting the new employee up to speed faster. One benefit to you is it demonstrates to your boss you show potential in leadership.

Leadership can also be by example. People see the ways in which you conduct yourself as an employee and coworker. It may be surprising just how much what you do and say are noticed by those around you. Why not take better control of what people see? Let them see what you want them to see. Not by being fake or hiding what you don't want seen, but by choosing actions that illuminate how you want to be seen. Consciously make these choices until these choices are natural and really are you.

Find and Obtain Skills Needed

> *"I use internet resources, websites, and online tools. Sign-up for blogs and read articles. Network with others and ask questions of coworkers and keep notes for references. I have gained a tremendous amount of knowledge by asking questions of my coworkers that have more experience than I have."*
>
> *- Ellen Coppler*

Keeping up to date on skills is something of benefit for most if not all jobs. It certainly is for the technical field that I have been a part of. Technology changes so fast, a technology professional must be aware and learn new technologies. In fact, there are so many new technologies and methods being released, it is impossible to even come close to mastering them all. Being selective is equally important as keeping up to date.

> *"I am blessed to work for a public school district. There are several procedures in place. New hires are assigned a mentor, and my mentor did a very good job of meeting with me and helping me both in my professional duties and navigating the culture of the organization. We also have professional development workshops, both required and optional. I have always attended more than the required number of workshops, and look for the ones that will help."*
>
> *- Bradlee Clegg*

Even if you don't work in the technology field, new ideas and methods are likely available in your field. What could learning a new method mean for your current job? Your future career?

First identify what new methods, technologies, courses, training opportunities, and certifications are available in your particular field. Rank these opportunities based on how much benefit they offer you in your current job, or in any future job you hope to obtain within the company you are currently at.

Then, be selective. Certainly technology is not the only field with so many facets that one could not hope to master every nuance of every sub-discipline. Think about your current job as well as your career goals. Compare these against the list of areas within your field. Which ones would benefit you and your company most by advancing in? Focus on those and only those. This list of areas may change over time. Trying to keep up with all of them may become overwhelming and possibly cause burnout. Instead, stick to your list for at least a few months before adjusting the areas you target. This will help keep you on track. It is very easy to see many areas as being needed to expand your career and to start trying everything you come across. This can quickly lead you to feeling ineffective at any of the areas and certainly not the core set you want to be focusing on currently.

> *"There [are] a number of places where one can find information and/or training. I have taken classes and earned a degree from a local college. Even reading articles on social media sites such as LinkedIn, and other industry of choice related websites and blogs. I have also obtained subscriptions to industry related magazines, ebooks and other publications to gain knowledge. Another resource would be to join clubs or groups that are related to the field that the employee works in (and you may even make a few friends along the way)."*
> *- Rebecca Elliott*

Go through the sources for information and training you built and start picking out the ones that best fit with the areas you determined are most important right now.

Be realistic as you build your list of information sources. Think about how many hours you can reasonably devote to training each week or each month. Are there training options your employer would allow you to complete during working hours? Are there even options your employer would be willing to pay for?

Work out a plan that includes regular training each month of some form. If your employer is willing, your plan could also include specialized training you could attend annually. These usually involve travel, extended stays, and expenses, so be sure to get all this pre-approved from your manager and see what the company is willing to pay for before you commit to the training event.

> *"There are tons of sites providing online classes and tutorials on most professional topics or disciplines. Talking to your manager about how they got where they are and what suggestions they have for you to improve would be an excellent starting point as well. Ask them what would make yourself become invaluable to them as an employee, and then strive to accomplish that."*
>
> *- C.J. Gonzalez*

Keeping yourself up to date within your field is crucial to keeping yourself marketable both at your current employer and future companies you wish to one day apply to.

Think Like Managers Would to Understand What Needs To Be Done

> *"Find a 'mentor' type of person to whom you look up to professionally. Ask your supervisor for constructive feedback regularly - not only during evaluations. Volunteer for projects that are outside your knowledge/comfort zone. Take a personality test to determine how your personality type functions in work environments - leverage the 'good' and seek to improve the 'not so good'. Read 'The 7 Habits of Highly Effective People'."*
>
> *- April Scrimger*

For more information on related resources like The 7

Habits of Highly Effective People by Stephen R. Covey mentioned above, visit www.successlifter.com/the-successful-employee.

Have you ever felt management views your work completely different than you or your coworkers do? Do managers seem to seldom understand the complexities and difficulties you face in your daily work?

Managers and employees don't necessarily always think the same way about the work that needs to be done. This isn't to say managers or employees are wrong in their views of what a job is or should be. It just means they have different expectations placed upon them by the company and therefore may view a job from different perspectives.

This is a critical understanding to explore further as an employee. How you relate to and understand your manager can have a large impact on how you do your job and the value you draw from your work.

Understanding how your boss and other managers in the company think on the job is a large enough topic in itself that it deserves more than just this section. We will touch on some areas of difference in thoughts between employees and managers here. However, covering all these details is outside the scope of this book. For a more thorough understanding of how your manager thinks on the job check out the next book in The Successful series, The Successful Manager. You can learn more about The Successful Manager at www.successlifter.com/the-successful-manager.

A new office chair. Casual dress days. A company paid special training event you found. Flexible work hours outside those the company typically offers. These are just a few of the possible perks employees may approach their manager to request, many of which may be no problem for the manager to approve. Some may not get approved. When a manager does not approve a request such as one of these it can be frustrating as an employee. It may even limit an employee's ability or freedoms within their specific work environment. It can lead to frustration and reduced work satisfaction. Something to keep in mind when such a request is rejected is why. Why was it rejected? We can jump to many conclusions about why it was rejected, many of which may be far from reality. If you aren't sure why, ask. If approached in a professional manner, most well-intentioned managers will likely disclose the reason for their decision. If your manager chooses not to explain, there may be more complex factors at work than you are aware.

If you work with others on your team, your manager has to balance these requests among the requests of all the others on the team. This ensures a more balanced work experience for everyone on your team.

Company resources or policies may be another factor entering into your manager's decision process. There may already be clear guidelines in place your manager must adhere to that would conflict with granting your request. Budget concerns the company is currently facing may also play a part in the decision.

Knowing the reason for the denied request can also serve to identify if the request could never be fulfilled or just can't be filled right now.

As employees it is very easy for us to find ourselves in a day-to-day work mentality in which we work to complete the task at hand with little regard for what the next task is or what these tasks lead to ultimately. The task itself may even be the only job we need to focus on. Working on an assembly line making the same auto part each day could easily place someone into this type of mindset.

First of all, there is nothing innately wrong with having such a mindset if it is not reducing your effectiveness at your job. But your manager may be thinking several tasks or projects ahead or how this task or project fits into overarching company objectives you may not be aware of. Your manager may be thinking about work load balance across your team. Understanding this fundamental difference in how your manager looks at your work versus how you look at your work will better prepare you for surprises - surprises such as a shift in your work to a new project or being moved to a factory machine you have never used, even though you have a solid understanding of the machine you had been using for the prior six months.

Remember that part of your manager's job is to provide a compelling, engaging, and rewarding work environment for his or her assigned employees. Granted, your manager must also ensure productivity. He or she may seem to overlook improving the work environment but your manager should be viewed as one of your primary advocates within your organization. Think of your manager in this light and try to understand the struggles your manager faces daily. This could build rapport and lead to improving their view of your work situation.

Take Opportunities Even If Uncomfortable

> *"Don't let the fear of not knowing something hold you back from learning or trying something outside of your wheelhouse."*
>
> *- Matthew Donaldson*

In an earlier section where we looked at owning mistakes, we talked about seeing opportunity in those mistakes. Opportunities come in many forms. Mistakes or bad situations you find yourself part of are ways to find opportunities. Any time some terrible major event happens at work that you see or are part of, ask yourself: What opportunities are being presented along with the problem?

Problems and failures don't have to just be negative.

It may take some time and practice to adopt such a mindset. It can be hard to stifle emotions as they well up in the heat of the moment, fighting to put out some type of emergency. But it is valuable to learn this skill.

When you are in the middle of fighting the emergency, be sure to take down some notes. Mental notes are okay if you can't write them down, but writing this out will be best. It can be hard to remember details from a tense situation after the fact.

Take notes on anything that may be helpful. What seems to have caused this? What are the ramifications of this issue? What are some ways to temporarily stop or lessen the negative effects of the issue? What are some ideas for a more permanent solution to prevent this from happening again?

Some of these questions you will need to answer after the issue is fixed and you have some time to think through all the aspects. But don't wait too long. The sooner after the issue you work through questions like these, the better your chances of capturing all the details you picked up on.

This is a Root Cause Analysis (RCA). In case you are unfamiliar with RCA, it is the act of analyzing an incident with the intent of identifying the impacts resulting from it and especially of finding the underlying cause that brought this about. I have provided a sample RCA form for you to use. You can access it with the book bonus materials at www.successlifter.com/the-successful-employee. You have full permission to reproduce and use this form as-is or modify it to meet your needs or your company's needs.

Waiting for a problem to come up isn't the only way to extend yourself into something new. A need within your company could be a project waiting to be recognized. Many times people will continue doing something the way they always have rather than thinking about an easier way to accomplish the task. This is not by any means a criticism. The phrase "if it ain't broke don't fix it" does have some merit. However, I suggest a slightly different version of that phrase. "If it works the best possible way already leave it alone, otherwise, what can improve?" This is a very different viewpoint. It borrows something from both ends of the scale.

One side of the scale is the phrase "If it ain't broke don't fix it". To me this phrase implies a blind trust that the current system is the best one possible. It goes right along with "That is how we have done it for years." That may be true, but years ago there might not have been the resources of today. Giving no room for consideration of a different approach is placing more value on the method than where it belongs - on the outcome.

The other end of scale also places more value on the method than the outcome, but from a much different perspective. Instead of being married to a single method there always must be something better. "The grass is always greener elsewhere" may be a fitting phrase here. If it is new and revolutionary it must be better, right? Not always. The newest idea or scheme for doing something may work very well in some instances but not others. Simply trying something new because it is new isn't enough to warrant departing from a tried and true method. This may seem like I am giving you conflicting advice, but bear with me a moment.

Both the methods above are approaches I have seen in business today. If you think a few moments on it, can you come up with a few examples of each of these either in your working experience or just by observing trends in society?

What is really important? Is it the method? Is how we do a thing first and foremost? No, the outcome is what we are after. That is the goal. The objective. The reason we are trying to figure out what method to use.

Now, that being said, I am not promoting the idea of the ends justify the means. If the outcome is the only importance then it doesn't matter what we do as long as we get the outcome. That is a dangerous statement and one we need to identify for what it is. This would open all sorts of immoral and illegal activity, none of which we should even give a moment's consideration. The outcome is not the only thing but it is the main focus. A mantra in this case may be something like, "The outcome is our primary concern as long as obtaining the outcome is by just and prudent methods."

Be outcome-minded not just method-minded. This is the balance we are after between the two ends of the scale. Here is a simple example to illustrate being too fixed on method at either end of the scale.

If you always visit your sister by car because she lives in another state your method is to "use your car." Your outcome is to "visit your sister." When your sister moves to a house down the street from you your method, "use your car," still works perfectly well. In fact, it is even more efficient than before as you are using far less gasoline. Placing value on the method over the outcome you would continue to drive and never question the method. This is how you did it for years. It worked then and it still works.

Now if you were too focused on trying any new method that comes along, you may have considered walking but not considered the fact that the state you live in has cold and icy winters. Throwing caution to the wind, you decide to switch methods, having seen a new opportunity. However, the trip is treacherous through deep snow and you fall three times on ice before arriving at your sister's house.

The more balanced approach I mentioned would look at other options. Noting the sidewalk that spans between both your and your sister's house, you may consider a new method to try. Walk. But decide to try the new method in the spring once weather permits. Perhaps you try the method out and find it takes a bit longer but it does not use the resource of your car and provides you exercise as well. You compare the methods and find more benefits to walking than driving and the outcome is still achieved using either method. Thus, you decide to switch your method. At least in good weather.

This is a very simple example. But the application can be made to a real method you see used at work. How the printing press is used today at your publishing company. The steps you go through to generate that report every week. Are the methods used for years still the best possible methods that can be used today? Maybe the answer is yes. But asking the question is how you find those that can be improved.

> *"Say 'Yes' to assignments that seem overwhelming or out of your wheelhouse. They are all a learning experience and you wouldn't be asked (or God wouldn't have put them in your way) if you didn't have the capability. Lastly, don't be afraid to travel, take a job away from your home, move your family somewhere else. You can always come home, but the opportunity to do something great may not come your way again."*
>
> *- Fran Mosher*

Always Know What Areas to Work on Improving

Do you know what areas of your job you are really good at?

Do you know what areas of your job you could do better with?

These are two questions you should ask yourself regularly. Know your strengths. Document those strengths with examples showing you demonstrate key qualities important to your company. Don't just stop with your strengths, though. Know areas you could use improvement. Document these too. Don't look at this second list as a negative that brings you down for not being good enough. This list will help you build up in these areas. It also shows your boss you are being realistic. Everyone has areas they can improve in. One duty a manager has is to know the areas each person on their staff can do better in and provide a means for them to improve. So, this list will be very valuable to your boss.

Go through each of the items on this list that need improvement and write down some ideas of what things you could do to improve on the area. Are there training courses that would provide you the information needed to improve in the area? Are there free resources available on the internet or even at your company that you would benefit from? List as many ideas as possible.

Now rank your top two or three ways to improve in each of the areas. Which one provides the best improvement? Which one is easiest to implement with little or no cost? Decide which ones should make it to the top of the list.

Also, go through the list of areas you could improve on and write down how it would benefit the company if you were to improve in these areas.

After this, pull out the top few areas you want to improve in over the next quarter and put these in an organized document you can present to your manager. Be sure to include the benefit each would have for the company, the ideas you have for improving on them, when you expect to have completed implementation, and any cost associated with training.

Now you are ready to set up a meeting with your manager to discuss your ideas for improving the work you do for the company. Be sure to bring the document you put together and be ready to talk through it. Your manager will likely want to see what kind of return on investment the company can expect in any training or other expenditures needed for you to complete your objectives.

Be prepared that your manager may not approve all of your ideas. Your manager may even alter some of the ideas. Still, be confident that you are trying to better yourself for the company's sake as well as for your own career.

To make this easier, please see the template I included with the book bonus material for how to research and document these areas to improve on. You can get that information at www.successlifter.com/the-successful-employee.

Earlier in this book we talked about looking for training to improve the work you do. But as we discussed above, training isn't the only way to improve in areas you are looking to shore up. Here are some ideas for finding tips and advice to improve on the areas you are interested in:

Internet search

The internet has a wealth of ideas and advice in various areas. Do some searches online to see if you can find some useful tips in any of the areas you are looking into. You may even be able to find a newsgroup devoted to your area of interest where you could post some specific questions you are looking for answers to.

Depending on the area you are looking to improve on, you may not need to restrict your searches and questions to only your profession. Many areas bridge across various professions.

Other employees

Observe other employees at your company. Some of them may have developed strengths in the areas you are looking to improve in. Ask them how they were able to improve in those areas and how you might do the same.

Asking your manager

See if your manager has suggestions on ways you could improve in the areas you want to focus on. If asking your manager for these suggestions seems too awkward try asking a manager in another department.

> *"Utilize career building websites such as LinkedIn. Be organized, search ways to organize your day and use your time more wisely. Tackle the most difficult tasks when you're at your best (are [you] a morning person or more alert in the afternoon?). If you have a lot of meetings research ways to become a more effective mediator [for] more effective meetings."*
>
> *- Ellen Coppler*

Keep Aware of Direction of Business

Where is the company heading? It shows management you have an active interest in the organization you work for and care about the success and mission of the company. Also it helps you better understand the shifting future landscape that could be coming for you.

Follow them in the news. Read any corporate newsletters. Ask appropriate questions to management to get a better feel for the future direction.

10. ADVANCE YOUR WORK

"Try and make your job enjoyable. Be engaged, get involved and stay positive."
- *Ellen Coppler*

"Be realistic in setting your path, but don't be afraid to stretch yourself. Balance the practical needs of you and the organization with some of the idealism and sense of wonder that can sustain you. Ultimately, the answers to a professional development path is set by practical considerations, but sticking to the path requires you to maintain that sense of purpose and personal leadership to sustain you."
- *Torin Lucas*

No matter if you are just starting your career journey with a vast future ahead of you or you have been at this a while, there are always opportunities around you to step up your game. Always find ways to stand out among the crowd. While many fields are very competitive, it IS possible to stand out. This book set out several methods for doing just that. Now it is up to you. What will you do with the information you just read?

Before you even set this book down, really think about what you will do next to advance your work. Don't let this book be just a short-term inspiration. Chart your course. Pick three areas you want to focus on over the coming months and write them down before you go on with your day.

Build your roadmap to being the employee you want to be; let's do this together! Check out www.successlifter.com/the-successful-employee. You will find bonus material to this book and more information all geared to helping you become the success you envision.

I look forward to seeing you there and wish you the very best possible success in your journey.

<u>Let's do this</u>!

The Successful Employee

REFERENCES

Adams, Susan.
> Forbes,
> https://www.forbes.com/sites/susanadams/2013/10/11/the-10-skills-employers-most-want-in-20-something-employees/#6e3284576330.
> 11 October 2013.

Amazon Benefits.
> Amazon,
> https://www.amazon.jobs/en/benefits.
> Accessed 3 August 2017.

Bennis, Warren.
> Wikiquote,
> https://en.wikiquote.org/wiki/Warren_Bennis.
> Accessed 31 August 2017.

Bolinger, Julie.
> Interview.
> 28 June 2017.

Coppler, Ellen.
> Interview.
> 14 July 2017.

Clegg, Bradlee.
> Interview.
> 13 July 2017.

Donaldson, Matthew.
> Interview.
> 23 June 2017.

Elliott, Rebecca.
   Interview.
   13 July 2017.

Gonzalez, CJ.
   Interview.
   16 July 2017.

Grenzicki, Michael.
   Interview.
   14 July 2017.

"How to Get a Raise."
   Wall Street Journal,
   http://guides.wsj.com/careers/managing-your-career/how-to-get-a-raise.
   Accessed 13 June 2017.

HIPAA.
   U.S. Department of Health & Human Services.
   https://www.hhs.gov/hipaa/for-professionals/privacy/index.html.
   Accessed 21 August 2017.

Lucas, Torin.
   Interview.
   3 July 2017.
   Marie, Savannah.

"10 Ways to Avoid Being a Yes Man",
   https://addicted2success.com/life/10-ways-to-avoid-being-a-yes-man.
   Accessed 1 August 2017.

Merriam-Webster,
   www.merriam-webster.com/dictionary/character.
   Accessed 7 July 2017.

Mosher, Fran.
  Interview.
  7 July 2017.
  Nordstrom, Todd, et al.

"Is Swearing Appropriate At Your Work?",
  Forbes,
  www.forbes.com/sites/davidsturt/2015/03/19/is-the-f-bomb-appropriate-at-your-work/#6d979c5e48a2.
  19 March 2015.
  Otto, Michael W., et. al.

"Exercise for Stress and Anxiety",
  Anxiety and Depression Society of America,
  https://adaa.org/living-with-anxiety/managing-anxiety/exercise-stress-and-anxiety.
  July 2014.
  Quora.

"Why And Where Is Teamwork Important?",
  Forbes,
  https://www.forbes.com/sites/quora/2013/01/23/why-and-where-is-teamwork-important.
  23 January 2013.

Root III, George N.
  "Importance of Teamwork at Work",
  http://smallbusiness.chron.com/importance-teamwork-work-11196.html.
  Accessed 4 August 2017.

Rosa.
  "Retired and Now: No purpose",
  www.retirement-online.com/retired-and-now-no-purpose.html.
  Accessed 11 August 2017.

Safeguards Rules.
Federal Trade Commission.
https://www.ftc.gov/enforcement/rules/rulemaking-regulatory-reform-proceedings/safeguards-rule.
Accessed 11 August 2017.

Scrimger, April.
Interview.
29 June 2017.

Taylor, Ernest Randall.
Interview.
1 August 2017.

Torin, Matthew.
"3 Ways Owning Your Mistakes Will Make You Powerful."
Entrepreneur,
www.entrepreneur.com/article/232417.
24 March 2014.

Healthwise.
"Stress Management: Breathing Exercises for Relaxation."
WebMD,
www.webmd.com/balance/stress-management/stress-management-breathing-exercises-for-relaxation,
14 November 2014.

Williams, Kimberly.
"8 Companies that Pay It Forward."
kwlms,
https://kwlms.com/2014/09/20/4-companies-that-pay-it-forward.
20 September 2014.

Woodberry, Garrick.
Interview.
28 July 2017.

ABOUT THE AUTHOR

Cultivating success in life is a unique proposition for each person. We all have a different definition of what success means personally. It can be challenging to find what things will spark us to action instead of leaving us dreading Monday morning. All too often we try to find our course to success alone, it doesn't have to be that way.

Victor is an author, entrepreneur, and works in the computer software industry. In addition to writing about success he can be found at SuccessLifter.com, a productivity-driven resource providing inspiration and ideas for each of us to build the success in life that means most to us.

When not writing, Victor likes to exercise and watch great movies.

www.ingramcontent.com/pod-product-compliance
Lightning Source LLC
Chambersburg PA
CBHW070250230526
45470CB00002B/547